@DREAMWORLD PUBLISHING

WOULDN'T IT BE GREAT IF...

FIRST EDITION

Illustrations by Lyn The Alien
Poetry by Neal The Earthling

Library of Congress Cataloging-in-Publication Data

Library of Congress Control Number: 2023936832

ISBN 978-1-7353554-4-3 (paperback)
ISBN 978-1-7353554-5-0 (eBook)

Published by *Dream World Publishing™*
Oak View, California

www.NealTheEarthling.com

@NealTheEarthling

NOWHERE ELSE TO GO

As in life, climbing up can be scary.

We take a fall,
Feel a bit shaken.

Hesitate.

Question our own capabilities.

Reaching low,
Before, there is nowhere else to go.

Mental battles take us on a downward spiral.

Until...

Until we say,
Enough!

Enough of this,
Enough of that;
Enough of everything at last.

Finally discovering,
It's time to bounce back.

From high to low,
Low to high;
Gravity brings us full circle,
Until blast!

Blast, Blast, Blast!

We reach for the sky,
Push past boundaries never understood;
All in a flash,
Life happens so fast.

All in a flash,
Life happens so fast.

It's never too late,
To enter a state;
Where we can be great,
And change our fate.

Imagine what the world could be,
Imagine if we all were free.

WOULDN'T IT BE GREAT IF...

Written by Neal The Earthling

Illustrated by Lyn The Alien

WHAT IF...

WOULDN'T IT BE GREAT IF...

WARS DID NOT EXIST,
AND WE COULD COEXIST.

WE COULD REJECT TEMPTATION
FOR LIFE'S BEAUTIFUL CREATION.

EACH DAY WERE A CELEBRATION,
OUR VERY OWN CORRONATION.

Imagine if WE COULD BE ONE NATION,
TURN OUR BACKS ON IDOCTRINATION,
IGNORE FALSE INSUINUATION.

WOULDN'T THAT BE GREAT?

Wouldn't it be great if...
WE COULD TRANSFORM EMOTION INTO MOTION,
PUSH BACK AGAINST COMMOTION?

Imagine if WE COULD CHANGE THE NOTION,
THAT CHANGE NEVER HAS TO COME...

IGNORE WHAT WE'VE DONE,
WHAT WE'VE BECOME;
ALWAYS ON THE RUN...

From death,
Choosing ignorance over depth;
UNABLE TO TAKE A BREATH.

They say, "ignorance is bliss."

Believe this,
And life is what you'll miss...

Opportunities to grow,
A chance to know;
HOW TO GLOW,
BE PART OF THE SHOW.

Wouldn't that be great?

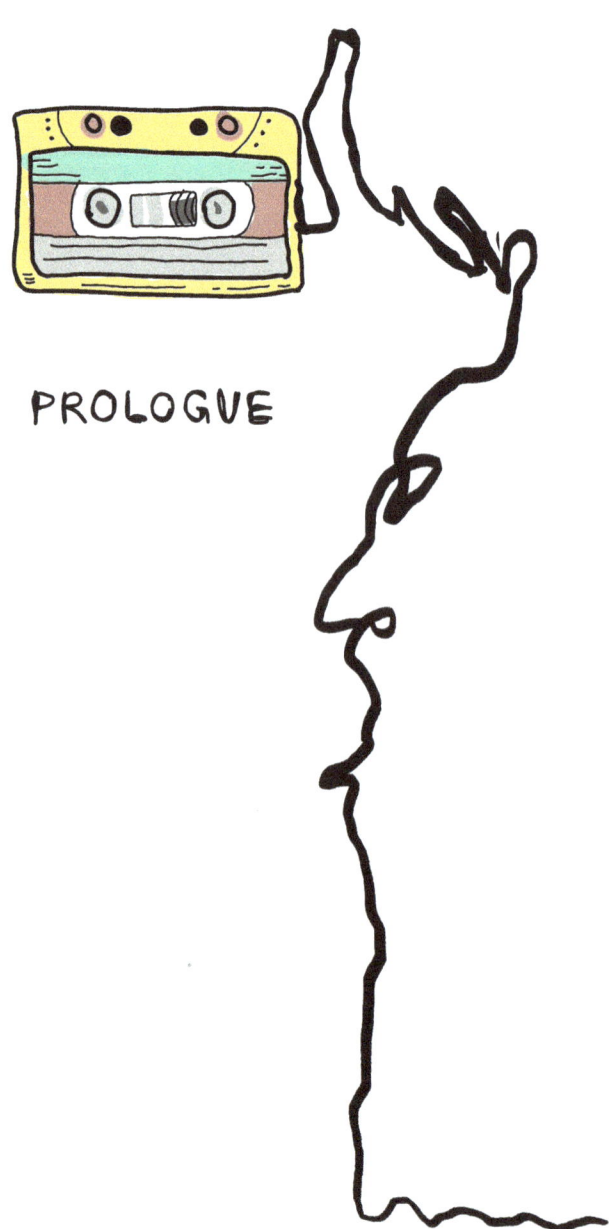

PROLOGUE

MY THOUGHTS

My thoughts have always been sincere,
Hopeful chatter from mind to soul,
The body, the spirit of what could be.

In 1996 at the age of 6,
I wrote my first poem,
Wouldn't it be great if…

At the time, all my mother,
a teacher could think was;
Wouldn't it be great if…

My son could read, write, and spell,
With good grammar, of course!

Oh, wouldn't that be great,
Wouldn't that be great...

Wouldn't that be great?

For me,
It was always about expression.

Whether a poem, a presentation,
Music, art, or jokes;
It had to be me.

True in form,
Sticking to ideals,
Facing adversity with honesty.

Often times,
This embodiment never saw the light of day;
Instead hidden in plain sight,
Cast aside by shadows,
Of who others wanted me to be;
Until it all changed.

Wouldn't it be great if…

MY DREAM

Wouldn't it be great if…

We could let go of EGO,
We could smile rather than frown,
We could laugh at life;
Wouldn't that be great?

Wouldn't it be great if…

Violence ceased to exist,
Kindness ruled the world,
Love not hate consumed us all;
WOULDN'T THAT BE GREAT?

Wouldn't it be great if…

Our happiness wasn't just a goal,
Our time wasn't taken away,
Our truth set us free;
Wouldn't that be great?

That would be great, but,
Greater than that would be…
Freedom to express our most authentic selves.

Oh, that would be great.

**THAT
WOULD
BE
GREAT!**

EXPRESSION

True expression would be great,
First, there lie many gates;
We must unlock, to unleash our fates.

If we could only enter a state,
Set the record straight;
Realize it's never too late,
To be great.

If only we could enter a state;
Where our senses abate,
Where we see things straight.

Why wait? Why wait?
WHY WAIT?

To change fate,
Before it's way too late;
TRANSFORMING OURSELVES
AND THE WORLD IN THE PROCESS.

WHAT IF...

What if…
What if?

What if…
What if?

WHAT IF WARS DID NOT EXIST...
Could we coexist?

WOULD SUFFERING PERSIST...
If we decided to resist?

What if we all worked together?
Would we be able to change the weather?

As storms become norms,
Climate reforms.

Fighting for resources,
Creating discourses…

Becoming scarce,
Competition fierce.

A struggle to survive,
Wishing to feel alive…

Frictions arise,
PEACE DIES.

Humanity tries,
But not hard enough;
Life becomes rough,
As lies take over.

Our future rests in this imbalance.

CAN WE FIND BALANCE?

If only…

WHAT IF?

What if…
What if?

What if we could?
What if we did?

Imagine getting rid,
Of humanities toxicity;
EGO-CENTRICITY...

Consumerisim,
False patriotism,
Surrealism....

That makes it hard to breathe,
Even harder to believe…

In hope over despair,
LOVE OVER FEAR.

What if…
What if?

If we could share,
If we could care...

IF WE COULD BE RIGHT HERE;
Instead of inside there...

IMAGINE THE WORLD WE'D SPARE.

WHAT IF...

WE REIMAGINED?

IMAGINE

Imagine what the world could be,
Imagine if we all were free.

Imagine the possibility…

Imagine, Imagine,
SIMPLY IMAGINE.

Imagine what the world could be,
Imagine if we all were free.

Free of fragility,
Free to regain stability.

Free of shame,
Free of taking blame.

We are one in the same,
Why take aim?

Tame the mental beast,
Enjoy life's feast.

To say the least…

Imagine what the world could be,
Imagine if we all were free.

Imagine what the world could be,
Imagine if we all were free.

Imagine the possibility…

To change outcomes,
Influence desire;
Work with the universe to conspire,
To light our inner fire.

Draw eyes ire,
Looking no higher;
An easy rider,
Outsider.

Free of despairs,
Knowing somebody cares;
Somebody hears,
What it is that scares.

Imagine what the world could be,
Imagine if we all were free.

IMAGINE IF WE ALL WERE FREE

Imagine the possibility...

Sharing in time,
Not yours or mine.

Dancing in rhyme,
On a rhythmic line.

Looking for precision,
Decision to decision.

A sign appears,
Its signal steers.

Distracted again,
This was not the plan.

Imagine what the world could be,
Imagine if we all were free.

Imagine the possibility...

Imagine, Imagine,
SIMPLY IMAGINE.

THE PUZZLE

Trapped in a vicious cycle…

A PUZZLE.

We are our own greatest puzzle.

We can solve it;
Or, we can absolve it,
Letting it consume us.

Moving pieces, hard to place;
THE TRUTH IS HARD TO FACE…

THE PAST EVEN HARDER TO ERASE.

The question is,
Where does each piece fit?

Shifting around,
Looking for solid ground;
When it's found,
Radiance will abound.

But, first, you have to address each wound;
That hollow sound,
Which ran aground**…**

ONLY FOUND WHEN IT COMES AROUND.

Feeling stuck, hung up…

Trapped by a vicious cycle,
You continue to recycle…

THE PUZZLE.

WHO IS THE PUZZLE MASTER?

Who is the forecaster?

Will things move faster?

Or slower?

Who is the knower?

Who is in charge?

MIND OR BODY;

BODY OR MIND…

Look inside, then unwind.

This is where you'll find…

THE WILL TO SOLVE THE PUZZLE.

WHO IS THE PUZZLE MASTER?

Who is the forecaster?

Will things move faster?

Or slower?

ENERGY

LEFT

UNTAPPED

Trapped in a vicious cycle…

The solution to this puzzle,
To all puzzles;
Is waiting.

THE PUZZLE REMAINS INCOMPLETE,
AS YOU GO ON, IN REPEAT.

Never admit defeat
I repeat, I repeat;
NEVER ADMIT DEFEAT.

THE PUZZLE IS WAITING TO BE SOLVED…

WHEN IT IS, SUFFERING WILL BE RESOLVED.

THE PUZZLE IS WAITING TO BE SOLVED…
WHEN IT IS, SUFFERING WILL BE ABSOLVED.

YOU

ARE

THE MASTER

AN ALTERED STATE

In an altered state,
Transformations wait;
Negative energy dissipates,
For what awaits.

Unlocking heaven's gate,
To a clean slate.

Open to the goal,
To connect with the whole.

CONNECTED CONSCIOUSNESS,
Also known as bliss.

Say goodbye,
To a past that won't be missed;
AN UNFOLDING TRYST,
Within our midst.

Step into an altered state,
Where change awaits,
Bad energy dissipates.

Beyond these gates,
Welcoming new fates;
As past abates,
A FUTURE WAITS.

AN ALTERED STATE...

Floating into the now,
Becoming the lightest feather somehow.

HOW? HOW?
HOW IS THIS POSSIBLE?

IMPOSSIBLE.

NOTHING'S IMPOSSIBLE.

EVERYTHING IS POSSIBLE IF YOU TRY.

Enter this altered state of mind,
Another kind of being...

SEEING TRANSFORMATION, INFORMATION;
NEW CREATION, INSPIRATION.

An altered state of mind,
The land beyond time...

WHERE ESSENCE CAN UNWIND,
WHERE SOULS CAN FIND...

WHAT LIFE IS LIKE WHEN IT'S NOT TIMED.

AN ALTERED STATE...

AN ALTERED STATE OF MIND,
UNABLE TO UNWIND;
THERE IS A LOT TO FIND.

Here's a reminder,
To see through each blinder;
Blocking clear view,
The way to breakthrough.

Annoyance,
Avoidance;
For clairvoyance.

Enter this altered state of mind,
To experience what awaits
When life is untimed.

CHANGE THE FORECAST

Change the forecast,
By being steadfast.

Have a blast,
Living in the present, yet passed.

THINK FAST.
THINK FAST.

FASTER...FASTER...
BECOME THE MASTER.

Now, don't think at all,
Let your body fall.

Release pent-up feeling,
For the unveiling.

Release tension,
Release any convention
Make this moment your best invention.

Redirect attention...

To change the forecast.

CHANGE THE FORECAST

Make it your own creation.
Make this creation a corronation.
Feel each new sensation.

Take inspiration from,
Become one;
Live to have fun,
Worship the Sun.

Don't run,
Don't come undone.

Be steadfast,
Have a blast,
And change the forecast.

CHANGE

CHANGE

CHANGE

CHANGE

CHANGE

CHANGE

CHANGE THE FORECAST.

CHANGE

CHANGE

CHANGE

 CHANGE

CHANGE

CHANGE

CAN WE OVERCOME?

CAN WE OVERCOME?

Can we overcome...
Can we overcome...

Can we overcome,
What we have done?

With each passing sun,
New life has begun.

Another chance,
To change our stance.

Another opportunity,
To try something different.

Can we overcome...
Can we overcome...

Can we overcome,
What we have done?

CAN WE OVERCOME?

Life used to be fun,
When we were no-one.

Then strung along,
By a need to belong…

Our choices were wrong,
Being led by the strong.

Opposites attract,
Is that a fact?

Others react,
Try to counteract.

THEY WANT EVERYONE TO BE THE SAME.

When you are different,
They blame…

Take aim,
Place shame…

A tireless game to defame.

Can we overcome…

Can we overcome,
What we have done?

Or, will we always run,
From the chasing sun?

What we choose,
We cannot excuse.

What we choose,
Win or lose.

Pressure's ruse,
Dwindling queues;
Soul's diffuse,
Ending blues.

CAN WE OVERCOME?

Yes, we can…

In this life-span,
We can begin again.

WE CAN
BEGIN AGAIN.

Again and again,
Again and again...

CAN BEGIN AGA

WHAT IF...

WE REDISCOVERED OUR IDENTITY?

IMAGE-BASED

Image-based,
A world defaced...

Left disgraced,
PEOPLE DISPLACED.

Refugees,
THEIR LAND IS SEIZED.

Refugees,
CROSSING EARTH AND SEAS

Searching for a home to call their own,
Never known, left all alone.

What life has shown them;
Is that they are not citizens…

Of any country or state;
Stuck in a state...

WHERE ALL THEY COULD DO IS WAIT.

While those in high places,
Separate people by races…

Split into classes,
Unruly masses.

And, for what?
FOR WHAT?

IMAGE-BASED...

AN IMAGE that will never satisfy them.

A world so thin,
One where nobody can win.

Image-based,
A world defaced...

LEFT DISGRACED,
People displaced.

And, for what?

For being able to show off,
While you drift off entirely…

FROM HUMANITY,
CAVING TO INSANITY,
WELCOMING CALAMITY.

A WORLD DEFACED.

...GE-BASED, A WORLD DEFAC...

...AGE-BASED, A WORLD DEFACED

...IMAGE-BASED, A WORLD DEFACED...

Ignoring cruelty,
Those ruled by decree…

Eventually unable to see,
Our common singularity.

Tying us together...

Together...
Together.

TOGETHER WE CAN WEATHER ANY STORM,
LETTING GO OF AN IMAGE THAT'S BECOME OUR NORM.

LET GO

LET GO

LET GO

PERFECT CREATURES

WE

ARE

ALL

FAR

FROM...

BEING PERFECT CREATURES.
What does perfect mean?

BEING PERFECT CREATURES,
Not being screechers
Or preachers…

ONLY BEING TEACHERS.
Only being teachers.

TEACH

TEACH

TEACH

Teach to be young...
Teach to have fun...

TEACH HOW TO BE LIKE THE SUN!

TEACH TO BE.
TEACH TO ME.

TEACH TO BE SOMEONE
AND NO-ONE...

AT

THE

SAME TIME.

TEACH TO BE HERE…
TEACH TO BE THERE…

**TEACH TO BE EVERYWHERE AND NOWHERE,
WHICH IS RIGHT HERE.**

Teach to be now,
DISCOVER OUT HOW.

Teach the world,
LEARN FROM IT.

Sharing your **ESSENCE.**
Sharing your **PRESENCE.**

BE LIGHT...

DON'T FIGHT.

SHARE WITH ME,
HOW TO BE...

SHARE WITH ME,
PLEASE SHARE WITH ME.

Share how to be beautiful,
HOW TO BE BRIGHT...

HOW TO TAKE FLIGHT,
Into a starry night.

EVERYTHING TURNS...

OUT ALRIGHT.

AIMLESS,
ENDLESS;
VAST AND WIDE,

TAKE ME TO THE OTHER SIDE...

Where I understand what it means to glide,
FLOW LIKE THE SHIFTING TIDE.

Moved by its current,
Blown by gentle wind;
Desire thinned,
Attachment dimmed.

Their memories left histories,
Once mysteries…

Experiences remained.

Neither looking backward
Or forward,
ONLY TOWARD…

What's here
In this present moment,
FREE OF ATONEMENT.

Sorrow.

Despair.

Pain,

Fear...

Sorrow.

Despair.

Pain,

Fear...

Calm and cool;
RELEASED FROM IT ALL,
HERE STANDING TALL.

THE WORLD YOU KNEW BEGINS TO CRUMBLE AND FALL.

BORN AGAIN, YOU START TO CRAWL.

AGAIN, YOU START TO CR

Walk,

Run…

Sprinting on by
SOON YOU'LL FLY;
Shed a tear, cry...

For everyone still suffering,
Showing compassion to them all...

In free-fall,
Life at a stall;
Until my call.

48

In my presence, you'll put past behind,
In my presence, you will find...

LIFE UNTIMED.

Time unwinds, future rewinds,
THE PRESENT MOMENT FINDS YOU...

That part within you, you always knew could be true.

WHO ARE YOU?

WHO ARE YOU? WHO ARE YOU? WHO ARE YOU?

YOU NEVER KNEW.
UNABLE TO SEE THROUGH.

YOU NEVER KNEW

SPLIT PERSONALITIES

SPLIT IN TWO...

Split personalities,
Two different realities;
And mentalities,
As dualities.

Competing personalities,
Living in alternate realities.

WHO ARE YOU?

PUSH...

Push and pull,
This is the rule;
It is cruel,
It is not cool.

Which one will you fool?
Which one will be your tool?

PULL.

It creates a rattle.

Shaking our core,
Are we ready for more?

Trying to soar,
We hit the floor.

Which personality is my reality?
Which one will win?

OVERRULE.

I spin, I spin;
My skin is thin.

What's been has been,
They're both akin….

Born from sin,
I'll never win.

One in the same,
When they came;
They're both to blame,
It's easy to explain.

One lays claim,
The other wanes.

One replaces,
The other displaces...

And then, it erases.

One lays claim,
The other wanes;
Creates a midframe,
Driving me insane.

Like the rain,
It's a pain...

I can feign,
Try to tame...

Who's to blame?

Better yet,
What's to blame?

Is it shame,
From where it came?

Is it fame,
From where it came?

FAILURE POURS.

This drive for more,
More and more;
My personality tore,
Me far from shore...

What's there left in store?

I hit the floor,
Will I ever soar?

Losing my core,
A negative score.

Spreading spores,
Failure pours.

FAILURE POURS.

SPLIT...

PERSONALITIES.

Split personalities,
Two different realities;
And mentalities,
As dualities.

SPLIT...

PERSONALITIES.

MY NAME

WHAT IS A NAME?

I hear my name,
Is this a game?

I hear my name,
WHO'S TO BLAME?

Why should I care about my name?
We're all the same, time to reframe.

What is a name? What is a name?

WHAT IS OUR AIM?

HELLO.

HELLO?

HELLO!

So much value placed,
So many souls displaced…

Even more, erased.

Spaced-out,
As EGO comes out.

My name brings shame
Or, my name brings fame…

**A CONTINUOUS GAME,
IT'S WAY TOO LAME.**

Someone calls my name again...

HELLO.

HELLO?

HELLO!

PLEASURE.

IS THERE SOMETHING TO GAIN
Pleasure or pain?

Will it drive me insane?
Or, will its influence wane?

After all, we are just a grain of sand.

Should I respond or act despondent?
Why should I be a correspondent?

Live on a single plane of existence,
Or act with resistance...

Instance after instance,
Glance after glance;
When we take a stance,
We take a chance.

PAIN.

Do it like this,
Do it like that.

Don't do this,
Don't do that.

ONLY WEAR THIS HAT!

Dictated to,
Unable to see through...

THE DECEPTION,
AN UNWELCOME RECEPTION.

I hear my name,
Is this a game?

I hear my name,
WHO'S TO BLAME?

Time to reframe.
Time to retrain...

Before a stain,
Becomes my grain.

I WILL NOT LOSE MY BRAIN!

WHAT IS MY NAME?

What is my name?
We're all the same.

WE'RE ALL THE SAME

63

Who am I?
I do decry.

Who am I?
Oh, how time flies by.

Who am I? *Who am I?*
WHO AM I?

Why? Why? Why?
WHY DO YOU ASK?

IS THIS A TASK?

Why do you ask?
Why does it matter?
Why should anyone care?

You look at me,
Wonder who you are;
Looking far,
To a bright blue star.

Calm like the ocean can be,
When not stormy;
Appreciating all its beauty.

Who am I in this moment?

WHO AM I?

WHO AM I?

WHO AM I?
WHO AM I?

I look to the sky,
Knowing the answer is not nearby.

WHO AM I?

WHO AM I?

WHO AM I?

WHO AM I?

WHO ARE YOU?

WHO ARE YOU

WHO ARE YOU?

WHO ARE YOU

WHO ARE YOU

Who are you?

When I look down on you…

Experiencing the world from a different point of view.

WHO ARE YOU?

CHANGE YOUR POINT OF VIEW.

LOOK,

SEE...

DON'T TELL ME

You don't know, do you?
You don't know what you don't know;
You only know what you do…

IF YOU CAN'T CHANGE YOUR POINT OF VIEW.

DON'T TELL ME.

LOOK,

SEE.

CHANGE YOUR POINT OF VIEW.

I AM YOU...

You ask me who I am…
I can be anyone.

Crossing any sea,
No matter how big it may be...

Or, even how far;
Even if…

I have to take a rocket
TO THAT BRIGHT BLUE STAR.

Who are you?
I am you.

I am you,
You never knew.

YOU NEVER KNEW.

I AM YOU

WHAT IS TRUE?

Who am I?
I am you.

Who are you?
You misconstrue.

Who are you?
YOU'VE GOT NO CLUE.

Your name game;
I'll call it a game…

Eliminate the name,
And, we're all the same.

Part of the universe,
Our name is our curse...

Let it burst,
Discover what's worse.

NOBODY KNEW.

TRAPPED

TRAPPED

TRAPPED

Saying we are this and that,
Playing tit for tat;
Living in a habitat,
Where we've become fat....

Or, that...

Tied to one hat,
Our mind becomes trapped.

TRAPPED

TRAPPED

TRAPPED

WE ARE ANYTHING.

Set it free,
Then you'll see…

Discovering you are nothing,
But, something…

Becoming anything and everything...

Transforming in a vortex,
Where our natural reflex, is suspect.

Open eyes reflect,
What we can't detect.

WE ARE EVERYTHING.

IDENTITY

Infinity,
Natures decree,
Endless possibility.

What will happen?
Does one know;
Find your glow,
And, it will show.

Infinity,
Natures decree,
Endless possibility.

IDENTITY

INFINITY

INFINITE

INFINITY

IDENTITY

Lost in space,
You can't retrace...

A ghost, left without a trace.

Now in place,
This present grace;
An ever-changing face,
Universal race.

INFINITE

INFINITY

IDENTITY

WHO ARE YOU?

Who are you?
You never knew.

Who are you?
You had no clue.

Who are you? Who are you?
YOU ASK ME!

I am you,
I thought you knew…

Now, that you know
What's true;
Let that thought sit and stew.

Do it,
Damn it!

YOU ALREADY BLEW IT!

YOU BLEW IT!

CLOSE YOUR MIND.

Close your mind,
Don't let it be timed.

Unwind, unwind,
Become color-blind.

Release yourself from the bind,
A past and future to remind;
Moments left undefined...

KNOWING WE ARE ALL HUMANKIND.

WE ARE ALL HUMANKIND.

WE ARE ALL HUMANKIND.

WHAT AM I?

What am I?

Not who am I;
*But, **WHAT AM I?***

Am I a creature,
From feature to feature?

I AM…I AM…

Am I a sentient being,
Seeing through the fog;
To a point where hope springs?

I AM…I AM…

Able to see what that brings;
BEAUTIFUL THINGS.

WHAT AM I?

Bringing alive un-awakened dreams,
That's how it often seems...

Realizing there's more beneath each surface.

Streams of consciousness.

Beams of light.

Fissures of sound,
Where true essence is found.

Holes in the ground,
Where limitless power is unbound.

A MENTAL TOUGHNESS,
YOUTHFULNESS.

Vitality transforms reality,
Coming out through sensuality.

Worlds renew,
What came before askew;
SUFFERING CAN NO LONGER ACCRUE,
ONTO YOU.

What am I?

Not who am I;
But, ***WHAT AM I?***

Connected with each breath,
I AM FULL OF DEPTH.

With life's kiss,
There's nothing to miss.

THERE IS NO STRUGGLE.

What will come will come.
What will come will come.

Isn't it strange how each moment is change?

What was in the past has passed.
What was in the past has passed.

What will come,
The past undone.

Living for each moment,
Nothing can last…

AT LAST,
Free of suffering at last.

I AM HERE.
I AM NOW.

WHAT AM I?

I AM ALIEN

I AM ALIEN…
I AM AN ALIEN.

Not from a different planet,
But from a different state of mind.

All you've got to do
Is put one foot in front of the other.

Feed your attention,
Or transform intention.

Feed only what you need,
Or your brain will bleed.

Reject greed,
And where that may lead.

It takes one tiny seed,
For things to speed.

Don't read...

Don't read
Too much into things.

You see,
What this brings…

Assumptions;
Presumptive thoughts
As stillness rots…

Black spots.

Caught in a battle,
We feel a rattle.

Gone is peace of mind,
Behind this state of mind…

Is the sublime,
There is no time.

Free of stress,
Nothing left to address.

We create things,
Which bring sufferings;
Making it harder to overcome…

To undo,
What we have done.

What have we done to ourselves?

What we've done to ourselves,
We have also done to others.

I AM YOU, AND YOU ARE ME...

WHEN I HARM ME,
NEITHER OF US IS FREE.

I AM YOU.

Before your next choice,
Listen to your inner voice.

If you wouldn't wish it upon others,
Refuse to let it onto yourself.

Reject desire,
Raise yourself higher;
Only conspire,
To stoke inner-fire.

Defeating THE EGO;
Letting it go…

Making room to grow,
Space to show…

What it means to flow.

YOU ARE ME.

YIN AND YANG

YIN

I am YIN,
I am YANG...

Staying in the middle lane,
No need to explain...

I am YIN,
I am YANG.

Yin and Yang,
I make it rain,
On an open plane.

Plain as can be,
Painlessly;
Stress-free,
Life is lovely.

I am YIN,
I am YANG...

Staying in the middle lane,
No need to explain...

I am YIN,
I am YANG.

YANG

Balanced,
Equal,
Mind-uncharged...

Still in place,
Mind-replaced.

The past erased,
The future displaced.

EGO encased,
Our story untraced.

YIN

YANG:

YANG

YIN...

YANG AND YIN.

YANG

YIN;

YIN

YANG...

YIN AND YANG.

Floating on a jet stream,
Living in a vivid dream.

BEING YIN,
BEING YANG.

What's there to explain?

Staying in the middle lane,
YIN and YANG.

STAYING IN THE MIDDLE LANE

I AM...

I AM...

I AM NOT EMPTY.

I AM NOT A VAST DARK HOLE,
BLACK INSIDE...

I WILL NOT HIDE,
I AM OPEN-WIDE.

I AM FULL OF LIGHT;
Deep inside, brighter than bright.

I am willing to fight,
To radiate light.

I AM WILLING TO FIGHT,
TO RADIATE LIGHT.

I AM NOT UPTIGHT,
I won't act in spite.

I AM...

I've never been quite there,
With my gift to see clear...

It's only when I share, myself;
That I can hear,
Released from fear.

I AM FEARLESS...

Nothing can scare me;
Nothing can break me.

I AM AWAKE,
I AM NOT FAKE.

I AM...

AWAKE,

NOT FAKE.

I WILL **NOT BREAK**

I AM...

AWAKE,

NOT FAKE.

You may be shocked by the way I talk;
That's because…

I AM AS HARD AS A ROCK.

Nothing can shock me;
I AM HARD AS A ROCK.

Solid, massive, dense;
Stuck in present-tense.

I am as strong as any gravitational pull,
I follow no physical rule,
I play it cool.

Connected by every sense…

HEARING,
SMELLING;
TASTING,
SEEING.

I AM...

This is my gift,
I use it to uplift…

There's nothing empty about it.

I AM...

I AM FULL OF LIGHT.

I AM THE WHITE LIGHT,
TWINKLING IN A DARK NIGHT.

I AM SUPER BRIGHT.

I AM...

A sight for sore eyes…

Reflecting into your eyes,
Things you'll never despise.

I AM WISE.

Rising above,
Come push or shove…

I AM FULL OF LOVE.

LOVE, LOVE, LOVE…

I AM LOVE.

THAT'S WHAT I AM.

I AM LOVE.

I AM LOVE.

I AM LOVE.

I AM LOVE.

WHAT IF...

WE TOOK RESPONSIBILITY?

AN ENVIRONMENT CAN BE

An environment can be…
What we make it out to be.

INTOXICATING OR SUFFOCATING;
STIMULATING OR DEPRECIATING;
ENHANCED OR ENTRANCED.

What is your environment like?

Its surroundings…

THE AIR,
THE COLORS;
THE SMELLS,
THE ENERGY.

Is it full of SYNERGY or MISERY?
Do you feel UPLIFTED or DOWNSHIFTED?

DRIVEN WITH VISION;
Or, DEPRESSED, LEFT UNIMPRESSED?

The environment we find ourselves in,
Is where our happiness can begin.

Sink or swim;
Dull or sharp;
Pungent or odorless…

Our experience influenced by this.

Will, you miss it,
When it's gone?

Or, are you ready,
For a new dawn?

With a fresh perspective,
Comes a new objective.

Hearing different sounds abound,
Discovering what there still is to be found.

Will it astound you?
Will it ground you?

Has it found you?
Pulled you out of the blue?

Will it renew you?
Bring back fleeting youth,
To rediscover truth?

WHAT DO WE WANT?

WILL IT HAUNT?

An environment can be,
Eternal life for you and me...

To treasure and take pleasure, in,
Remembering where life does begin.

What is your environment like?

WILL IT HAUNT?

WHAT DO WE WANT?

WHO'S TO BLAME?

WHO'S TO BLAME?

Traffic,
Congestion…

Pollution,
Collusion.

What is real?
What is not?

Are we bought,
By what we're taught?

Once upon a time, our ancestors fought…

Now, they've given up.

Any gains,
Few remains…

Lasting stains,
Little grains.

Victories won and lost;
A big toll, a bigger cost…

NOW, IT ALL SEEMS LOST.

They tossed it all,
Until our current fall.

Blaming,
Shaming...

Defaming,
Abstaining.

WHO'S TO BLAME?
This is not a game.

WHO'S TO BLAME?
They say it's all the same.

WHO'S TO BLAME?
They say this younger generation just wants fame.

They want to leave their name,
In a period that never came...

Without realizing they are no one,
When all is said and done.

WE ARE ALL ONE,
The setting sun will come.

The sum of us all
Is our true call.

If we fail to see this,
WE ARE BLINDED…

Blinded by false identity.

Blinded by piety,
A false deity,
Ignorant society.

Blinded by a false belief,
To bring relief.

Dead not alive,
How can we survive?

Who's to blame?
Who's to blame?

Don't just shame,
Give a name.

WHO IS TO BLAME?

WHO'S TO BLAME?

MASTER DISTRACTORS

DISTRACT,

REACT,

AN ACT.

Master distractors,
Nuclear reactors;
THEY ARE ACTORS,
Take advantage of factors…

That only serve themselves.

CHAIN REACTIONS
CAUSED BY THEIR DISTRACTIONS;
CREATING FACTIONS,
NEGATIVE ACTIONS.

Who do they serve?
Only themselves.

What do they serve?
They serve nothing.

THEY DESERVE EVEN LESS.

AN ACT,

DISTRACT,

REACT.

Preserving their own demise,
It's no surprise;
Telling lies…

THAT TOO MANY, SOUND WISE.

It's a disguise,
An act giving rise...

TO WHAT WE ALL DESPISE.

They feed off desire,
They never tire;
They go wire to wire,
Pulling us into the fire.

Creating division,
Through each incision;
Making the decision,
For revision.

Master distractors,
Nuclear reactors;
THEY ARE ACTORS,
Take advantage of factors.

Divide, Divide;
NOW I PROVIDE...

I may have lied,
At least I tried...

Where others died,
I defied.

Division through vision,
Obscuring, deterring...

DIVIDING AND CONQUERING;
PERSUADING AND DISSUADING;
CONSTANTLY DEGRADING.

Distract,
Distract,
DISTRACT!

THE ONLY ACT,
Free of any fact...

FREE OF ANY FACT.

No need to react,
That's how we counteract.

Master distractors,
Nuclear reactors;
THEY ARE ACTORS,
Detractors from the common good...

Knowing we all want to be understood.

109

DISTRACT,

REACT,

AN ACT.

Yet, there are NO FACTORS,
That cause THESE ACTORS;
THESE MASTER DISTRACTORS…

To act for anyone but themselves.

They're evil, you see,
Lacking any natural ability.

They're weak you see,
Lost in their own fragility.

Listen to the way they speak,
You'll see them as weak;
Unless you seek,
An unreachable peak.

If you are not looking for anything,
They have nothing to show;
After all, TO THEM…

IT'S ALL A SHOW.

AN ACT,

DISTRACT,

REACT.

They don't want anyone to grow,
They don't want anyone to glow...

This is what makes them go.

Sucking every last bit of oxygen from the room,
Leading their followers to impending doom.

We should ignore them,
Deplore them;
SILENCE THEM,
BY NOT RESPONDING TO THEM.

THESE MASTER DISTRACTORS,
Nuclear reactors;
Nearing their break,
Until the earthquake…

Then you'll see how fake;
HOW FAKE THEY'VE BEEN;
HOW THIN-SKINNED THEY ARE…

THEY ARE NOT TO BE TRUSTED.

Waiting to explode,
Better to let them implode…

THESE MASTER DISTRACTORS,
THEY ARE ACTORS.

HEAT-SEEKER

HEAT-SEEKER,
HEAT-SEEKER…

Missile fired,
Aim wired;
WHAT CONSPIRED?

Connection tired.

A speaker echoes,
SOUND FROM UNDERGROUND…

Will connection rebound,
Or run aground?

RD TO TELL, UNDER THEIR SPE

Masses of matter rush;
Reacting to alarm bells,
Spelling out doom…

We are left to assume.

The fume cloud,
Creates a crowd;
Chattering loud,
Nobody's proud.

HEAT-SEEKER,
HEAT-SEEKER…

You're making us weaker,
Noise reverberates from a speaker.

OMING OUT OF OUR SKIN.

Preaching doctrine,
Living in spin…

Truth thins,
Nobody wins.

AN EVIL GRIN.

Our minds illusion,
To reach a conclusion…

Trading discomfort,
For a safe comfort…

Easily indoctrinated.

Diffusing,
Confusing;
ABUSING OUR MINDS…

For one kind of thought,
We have been bought.

Caught up in conspiracy,
Scared by heresy…

Leaving mystery a mystery,
Forgetting our history.

Misled by distractions,
Causing over-reactions.

WEAPONS DRAWN...

Here it comes,
Missile runs;
Guns, guns, guns.

**Weapons drawn,
Our future gone.**

HEAT-SEEKER,

HEAT-SEEKER...

THE MASSES GROW WEAKER.

The heat we've been sold,
Turns gold into mold.

What these self-proclaimed prophets
Have sold, will make us fold.

As we transform from young to old,
We forget what it means to be bold.

OUR FUTURE GONE.

Heat-seeking followed;
Reaching a boiling point…

A POINT OF NO RETURN.

Nothing earned,
Less is learned.

Lies reach highs,
Endless cries we despise…

We fail to rise,
Welcome surprise;
We've turned into spies,
And become unwise.

Rewired,
As each missile is fired;
We are tired of this mess.

HEAT-SEEKERS,
LOUDSPEAKERS;
EGO CREATURES,
OVER-REACHERS…

NO TEACHERS.

HEAT-SEEKERS,
HEAT-SEEKERS.

YOU WERE IN A CULT

You are enough just the way you are.

Your were in a cult,
What was the result?

MIND ASSAULT.

Told you're crazy,
Your mind is hazy.

Belong,
Follow along…

QUESTIONS ARE WRONG!

The scripture is the word,
Any other way is absurd…

If you do,
You are disturbed.

You were in a cult,
The result?

A MIND ASSAULT.

YOU ARE ENOUGH...

A cult creates norms,
Culture forms...

BOUNDARY DEFORMS.

JUST THE WAY YOU ARE

WRONG.

WRONG,

WRONG!

Its leader takes power,
His followers cower…

To afraid,
Hidden they stayed;
Nobody to aid,
Barricade.

Longing to belong,
Following along…

To a singular song,
That's just plain wrong.

YOU

ARE

STRONG.

YOU WERE IN A CULT.

You were in a cult…
You escaped,
They raped.

Took control of your mind,
Making you blind,
Unable to find,
Courage to unwind…

The grip;
Its hold on you…

The past has you;
Until you renew.

Let it go,
Life will flow;
Continue to grow,

YOU WERE IN A CULT.

LOVE!

WHY FEAR?

NEVER SEE CLEAR.

IT WAS BRAINWASHING…
IT WAS DEVASTATING….

FRUSTRATING, AGGRAVATING…

What kind of world are we creating?

HATE!

WHY CARE?

SOON **TO DISSAPEAR.**

LOOK THROUGH...

Taxing on the soul,
Feelings of love swoll.

Were they true...
Or, a spell on you?

You knew, you knew,
To look from a different point of view.

See through;
Using this wider lens to cleanse…

Diminishing the past;
For a future yet cast.

DREAMS WILL COME TRUE.

You are perfect
Just the way you are.

Another star in the sky,
Waiting to fly…

Not allowing life to pass by,
Without wondering why?

WAS IT A LIE?

Am I crazy?
Am I, Am I?

HOW MANY TRUTHS DID I DENY…
To believe this big lie?

Who am I?

The cult can die.

I longed to belong,
But it was plain wrong.

Am I strong?

Maybe I'm wrong.
I don't belong.

WHO'S RESPONSIBLE?

WHO'S RESPONSIBLE?

We lose thoughts,
They take cheap shots...

Hope rots,
Mind-bots.

Unable to accept,
A new concept...

We look outside,
Our scope of view;
Hard to review,
As time flew.

World-wide problems grew,
Nobody could renew;
In our phones, we were stuck like glue.

WHO'S RESPONSIBLE?

Passing days,
Same old ways…

Wanting to blame,
Others for playing life's game;
Forgetting we are the same,
Ready, aim, fire…

Will the universe conspire?

Shooting for glory,
Leaving a mark on history…

Our own story a mystery.

WE'VE

LOST

THE WAY,

WHO'S RESPONSIBLE?

WHO'S RESPONSIBLE?

THE WAY

HAS BEEN

LOST.

Glued to moods,
Reacting to others' attitudes…

Creating battling feuds.

Fighting instead of uniting,
Writing on the wall…

Leading to an eventual fall,
Rejecting nature's call.

Free-falls,
Living stalls.

WHO'S RESPONSIBLE?

WE

ALL

ARE.

WHO'S RESPONSIBLE?

WE ALL ARE.

WE

ALL

ARE.

WHO'S RESPONSIBLE?

Forgetting inside,
We are stars…

Little balls of energy;
When connected, full of synergy.

But, we disconnected long ago,
Chose to forgo,
What we once did know.

**WE LOST OUR GLOW,
CAME OUT OF FLOW.**

Bringing down symbiosis,
With the world…

Breaking systems;
Synchronicity,
Currents of electricity.

Split wires,
Misfires…

Outliers,
Deniers.

Fighting over facts,
Each of us reacts…

Power distracts,
Pushes us off tracks.

We've lost our way,
Within each day;
Missing another sunray,
For EGO'S play.

In the end,
Who's responsible?

TELL ME, WHO IS RESPONSIBLE?

WHO

IS

RESPONSIBLE

WHO'S RESPONSIBLE?

WHO IS RESPONSIBLE?

WHO IS RESPONSIBLE?

WHO IS RESPONSIBLE?

WE

ALL

ARE.

We've made the planet unstable,
While we were able…

We are still capable,
If we take responsibility;
If we accept the truth…

ANYTHING IS POSSIBLE.

ANYTHING IS POSSIBLE

WHAT IF...

DRIVEN INSANE

Insane.
Crazy,
Life turns hazy.

Taking twists and turns,
It burns, It burns.

Goodwill earns,
Everybody learns.

In near-view,
That may not seem true.

Looking long,
This terror does not belong.

Am I wrong?
Tell me I'm wrong.

I DARE YOU…

Because I know what's true.

Looking through the glass mirror,
Fracturing, cracking,
never capturing…

What I'm unpacking.

Looking beyond,
A mellow pond.

Connecting with my bond,
To passivity….

Opening a cavity between each calamity,
THE PATH TO INSANITY.

HOPE,

COPE,

NOPE.

When the world seems lost,
Our moral compass the cost…

There is still hope,
Which makes it easier to cope.

NOPE,

COPE,

HOPE.

Presently,
It's hard to see…

In the future what could be,
Beautifully.

Serenity,
Rid of insanity…

Openly, honestly.

No act is in vain,
There's always potential to gain.

Potentialities,
New-found realities,
We convert into actualities.

Working together,
Changing the weather.

Untethered,
Free reign…

Rid of pain,
Driving us insane.

Aim high,
Not low;
Shine bright,
Now glow…

You never know,
You never know…

How each of our stories may go.

With passing days,
Endless possibilities to grow…

When things move slow,
Break into flow.

Cycle's of birth and death,
From breath to breath…

Signaling to our brain,
What's crazy,
Even more insane…

Nagging pain,
On this earthly plane.

LOSING OUR BRAIN...

Wishing for cohesion,
Searching for a reason...

An existence full of resistance,
Instance after instance.

It's plain to me,
An insane way to be…

Ridiculous decree,
That makes us angry.

Like a rotting tree,
Boiling to a higher degree…

Until reaching a point of no return,
Any possibility to discern,
Lost in return.

AN ENERGY DRAIN...

CRAZY,

LAZY,

HAZY.

Driven insane,
Drowning in pouring rain…

Caught in a rough current,
Of the abhorrent.

HAZY,

CRAZY,

LAZY.

HOPE,

COPE,

NOPE.

Evil,
Devil…

BE THE REBEL.

Rebel against an insane spell,
Don't let them tell,
Don't let them sell…

Dreams,
Nightmarish things…

Only brings,
Sufferings…

FROM WHICH NEGATIVITY SPRINGS.

DRIVEN INSANE.

Clinging to permanence,
Holding onto our contemporary existence;
When everything is impermanent.

CHANGE IS THE ONLY THING.

CHANGE

CHANGE

CHANGE

CHANGE

CHANGE

CHANGE

CHANGE

CHANGE

CHANGE

Everything changes,
Our universe rearranges;
Past identity, it estranges.

It may seem insane,
Even crazy,
But, the future is hazy…

Full of potential,
Which is exponential.

Exponential, our true potential.

NENTIAL, OUR TRUE POTE

145

EMOTIONALLY CHARGED

Emotionally tied,
Too much we cried.

Emotionally lost,
At such a cost.

Emotionally bought,
Our mind was caught.

Wrapped up in emotional ways,
Every day shady Grays.

Feeling astray,
We've lost our way;
Drawn by what people say,
We hope, and we pray.

An overcast outlook,
Present reality shook.

Eventually, the Gray goes away,
The shade cannot stay...

Clearing skies for a new sunrise.

An opportunity to rise,
Surprise awaits;
EGO deflates,
Invigorates.

Problems evaporate,
Eliminating our dire state…

The state of things,
The problem that brings.

EMOTIONALLY CHARGED.

Scared straight,
We face our fate.

FEELINGS ENLARGED...

ENERGY DISCHARGED.

LOSE,

REFUSE,

YOU CAN CHOOSE.

Refuse to be emotionally tied;
Refuse to be emotionally lost;
Becoming lost, at such a cost.

No longer can we be bought;
No longer will our character be distraught;
Caught up in things, more than what seems.

Connected or owned,
Are we cloned?

Murky or clear,
Wishing truth to be near;
If only we could see there,
Through our own fear…

Reality would tear,
As dreams reappear,
Watching problems disappear…

I swear, **I swear, I swear!**

Here is where,
When emotions scare;
Others show care,
And, we can share…

Helping us bear,
Emotionally charged air.

TRANSFORM EMOTION...

SPUN,

HUNG,

HEAD RUNG,

Emotion can cause commotion,
Or, it can cause motion.

WHEN

WILL IT

BE DONE?

INTO MOTION.

Stop, freeze, try to appease.

Move, prove, find your groove.

Released by emotion,
Or, caught by it.

Released by emotion
Or, caught by it.

Emotionally tied,
Too much we cried.

Emotionally lost,
At such a cost.

Emotionally bought,
Our mind was caught.

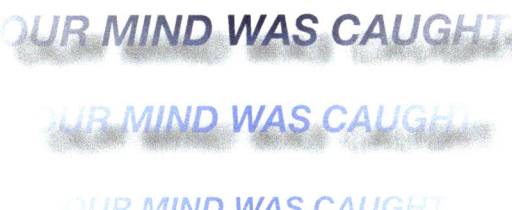

ANXIETY SOCIETY

Anxiety society,
Unable to gain sobriety.

Insecurity,
Driven by fear,
Never looking back,
In the rear.

It's our truth,
People smear.

It's hard,
To see clear.

We wonder where,
We wonder where.

Where o' Where o' Where o' Where...

Where are we going?
Why are things slowing?

How come nothing is flowing?
When will we start growing?

PAIN SO SEVERE...

Falling victim to evil's glare,
Trapped within its lair.

Causing a scare,
An empty stare...

Does anyone care?

ARE WE SINCERE?

Deep inside our heart,
Looking for a fresh start…

Parting from devilish ways,
Lasting for too many days.

Hope sways,
Our mind, our body stays…

EGO plays,
Triumph slays.

ANXIETY

SOCIETY,

HOUT SOBRIE

It took its toll,
All that it stole…

What remains, our loving soul.

SOCIETY

ANXIETY

We fell victim to every troll,
And, each soulful truth they stole;
Bringing about lull after lull…

Lows before highs,
Blows and cries.

Unable to escape,
Unable to find,
Unable to unwind...

From this heartbreaking bind,
Disconnected from mind.

ANXIETY

SOCIETY

Lost in anxiety,
Gone is sobriety.

Searching for meaning,
THE TRUTH IS SCREAMING!

ANXIETY

SOCIETY

WITHOUT SOBRIETY

Truth that does not speak,
The reality we seek;
As painful memories leak,
Going up instead of down creek.

SOCIETY

ANXIETY

Fighting the current,
We become abhorrent.

A torrent of power,
Makes us cower.

Pedals fall off our flower,
Light turns sour.

ANXIETY

SOCIETY,

ITHOUT SOBRIET

ANXIETY

SOCIETY;

SOCIETY

ANXIETY,

WITHOUT SOBRIETY,

This inability makes us feel weak,
Puts us on a losing streak…

Controlled by anxiety;
ANXIETY SOCIETY…

Unable to gain sobriety.

ANXIETY SOCIETY.

WHAT HAPPENED TO ME?

What happened to me?
I could not see...

Anxiety...
ANXIETY...

Another causality,
Of society.

Months gone by,
Where I...

Felt low, not high.

Days past,
My essence cast...

It moved fast,
Never letting a moment last.

This mind of mine,
It wanted to shine...

Stuck in a body that could never keep up.

Dragging,
Lagging behind;
Signaling to my mind,
To unwind...unwind...

What would it take to remind?

WHAT HAPPENED TO ME?

Where did I stray off the path?

You'd think it would be simple math.

Looking back now, we can laugh…

At our crazy society,
Separated from reality;
Drunk on anxiety,
Far from sobriety.

ANXIETY!

ANXIETY.

ANXIETY!

ANXIETY.

ANXIETY!

ANXIETY.

ANXIETY!

ANXIETY.

ANXIETY!

ANXIETY.

You see the world.
You see it all.

What we see may not be,
What it may be is anxiety;
Another casualty of society,
Waiting for sobriety….

Waiting,
Always waiting.

WHAT HAPPENED TO ME?

CONSPIRACY

Mysteriously,
Conspiracy.

Conspiracy,
Heresy.

"Hearsay," is what I say.

You hear what they say,
You act in dismay.

You hear what they say,
You look the other way.

Believe what is not,
Opposite of what you are taught.

You thought you were being smart,
You thought, "This is where I start."

Taking an opposing view,
To what may or may not be true.

You look for a clue…

You look for another clue…

Now, they've got you.

CONSPIRACY

CONSPIRACY

CONSPIRACY

Others thought they knew,
You did too.

CONSPIRACY

CONSPIRACY

CONSPIRACY

CONSPIRACY

CONSPIRACY

CONSPIRACY

CONSPIRACY

"I AM BEING INDEPENDENT."

"YOU ARE DEPENDENT."

OTHERS THOUGHT THEY KNEW

YOU DID TOO...

NOW, THEY'VE GOT YOU

Depend to upend,
In the end,
Refusing to bend.

Spending energy,
Consuming your mind;
Believing you'll find,
And truth will unwind.

CONSPIRACY

CONSPIRACY

CONSPIRACY

CONSPIRACY

CONSPIRACY

Against the grain,
You are all the same.

Trying to be…

To be free…

Think independently…

Nobody can tell you what may be.

Although, that cannot be…

THAT CANNOT BE.

You see.
You see.

CONSPIRACY

CONSPIRACY

CONSPIRACY

THEY HAVE THE ABILITY...

TO MAKE YOU SEE.

They have the ability,
To make you see.

They have the ability,
Of deceivability.

THEY HAVE THE ABILITY...

OF DECIEVABILITY.

Power,
Money;
WHO IS HUNGRY?

Morally bankrupt,
They corrupt.

Bad actors,
Using evil factors;
Some detractors,
Counteractors.

CONSPIRACY

CONSPIRACY

CONSPIRACY

CONSPIRACY

CONSPIRACY

ONSPIRAC

ONSPIRAC

CONSPIRACY

ONSPIRAC

Manipulative,
Duplicative…

Duplicitous,
Conspicuous.

Under their spell,
You accept what they sell;
Falling for the lies they tell.

You are receptive,
To take their perspective.

Your mind is blind,
Trying to be a different kind…

Of being, believing;
While receiving what's deceiving.

A RABBIT HOLE,

ANOTHER SOUL IT STOLE...

A rabbit hole,
Another soul it stole...

Spiraling down,
World flipped around…

Placed in the ground,
Conspiratorial sound...

When it's found,
Conspiracy crowned.

WHEN IT'S FOUND,

CONSPIRACY CROWNED.

Taking fiction,
Making it addiction;
A condition,
Of unwavering position.

"I will not be told what to believe."
"I do believe…I do believe."

"I believe what I can conceive,
No government will deceive."

If my mind can find it,
What's behind it...

What's behind,
Things to which my mind is blind.

I can untangle,
Understand their angle…

To control….

The masses.
Breaking them down by classes.

To control…
To control…

Another troll.

INDEPENDENCE THEY TOOK...

THEY

TOOK

UR INDEPENDENC

Independence they took,
Telling us where to look.

THEY

CREATED

UR DEPENDENC

TELLING US WHERE TO LOOK

174

ANOTHER DAY LOST...

Nobody will tell me
How the world may be;
I will make it reflect my personality…

Despite the reality.
Despite the reality.

If you agree,
They deliver decree;
I gladly disagree,
Create my own factuality.

OUR FREEDOM IT COST.

I

HAD

NO CLUE.

I think I knew,
What was true…

Truth is, I had no clue,
I just could not see through.

The wormhole,
Cyber troll;
Manipulations toll,
Heads roll.

Conspiracy,
Hysterically…

There is no mystery.

I

COULD

NOT SEE THROUGH.

176

Heresy,
Conspiracy.

Don't you see,
It probably cannot be?

This conspiracy,
It is not scientifically proven;
Just enemies trying to sow confusion…

Leading everyone into delusion.

This collusion against science,
This bad alliance…

Is the real conspiracy.

Something you will never see.
Something you will never see.

DIVIDE THE NATION

DIVIDE

DIVIDE

DIVIDE

DIVIDE

Divide the nation,
With chaotic creation...

Insinuation, infatuation,
With a sour sensation.

Recreate, repatriate;
HOW DID WE BECOME THIS EVIL STATE?

DIVIDE

DIVIDE

DIVIDE

DIVIDE

Imagination,
Loss of creation…

Isolation, defamation.

DIVIDE

DIVIDE

DIVIDE

DIVIDE

DIVIDE

DIVIDE

ALWAYS TIED, WE NEVER TRIED

We take sides,
Who decides?

We take sides,
Who provides?

Uninspired,
Our minds are wired.

Connected on a grid;
Where we swerve,
Skid,
Blow our lid!

No inspiration,
We've lost natural sensation;
Imagination and creation,
To indoctrination…

INDOCTRINATION TO A NATION.

INDOCTRINATION TO A NATION.

TRY.

WHY,

GOODBYE.

Conflation of ideas,
Separating us from roots…

Leaving scattered remains,
Which explains these depressing stains.

Scars, marks which cannot be forgotten…

Something feels rotten;
WHAT HAVE WE GOTTEN?

LIE

AFTER

LIE,

GONE AWRY.

WE'VE GOTTEN LIED TO...

We've gotten lied to, lied to;
Taught things untrue;
Fed misleading clue after clue…

Some knew, some knew…

I'M TELLING YOU,
I'M TELLING YOU!

LIED TO, LIED TO...

Separating from fact,
Honesty lacked.

Dividing the nation with insinuation,
A most powerful creation.

Infatuation,
Repatriation;
Separation,
From imagination…

INDOCTRINATION THROUGH ISOLATION.

VE COULD NOT SEE THROUGH

DIVISIONS.

COLLISIONS;

INCISIONS,

REVISIONS.

Misled by all the lies fed,
Thinking minds go to bed;
In a way, they are dead.

Turned off,
Shutdown,
Drowned...

A KING IS CROWNED.

OUR WORLD

FLIPPED

UPSIDE DOWN.

UR WORLD FLIPPED UPSIDE DO

DIVIDING THE NATION,

THEIR WORST CREATION,

Division,
Revision;
Incision of reality...

Subverting now,
Diverting how?

Distracting to divide,
False advertise to provide;
Until we all decried,
Divisions, they are wide...

WHEN WILL WE DECIDE?

WHEN WILL WE DECIDE?

WHEN WILL WE DECIDE?

WHEN WILL WE DECIDE?

WHEN WILL WE DECIDE?

WHAT WE HAVE IN COMMON

People focus on their differences,
More than their commonalities.

Why can't we set aside our differences,
To appreciate the things we have in common?

Why not bring people together,
Rather than splitting them apart?

Pushing for defiance,
To break our alliance.

From the news
Driving ratings,
To the world, we are creating...

I'm not sure anymore.

Everyone I meet is kind.

There are extremes on both sides.

When groups form,
Division becomes the norm;
The extreme knows,
And, it shows.

It starts with small divisions,
Followed by targeted incisions...

Then come revisions,
Before the collisions.

Violent clashes,
Corruption collapses;
Another mind thrashes,
Society crashes…

Death lapses.

DIVIDE,

THEY LIED.

DIVIDE,

WE DIED.

DIVISION,
INCISION...

REVISION,
COLLISION.

DIVISIONS THEY ARE WIDE.

We were deceived,
Because we believed.

WE WERE DECIEVED.

Now, we try to breathe...

Clean air,
That we shall share.

Kind love,
That we shall share.

Free belief,
That we shall share.

True words,
That we shall share.

DIRTY,

ROTTEN,

FOUL.

HATE,

IRATE,

IS IT TO LATE?

190

WHAT DO WE HAVE IN COMMON

HOPE,

BELIEF.

RELIEF.

FROM GRIEF

If we could put aside
Our differences…

To see, that we;
Have more in common
Then we think...

If we could stop,
If we could think;
Before we take another drink…

Blink a few times,
Expand our vision;
Beyond the television…

To end the division.

We think we are in a dream,
A nightmare is more how it seems;
Maybe, it's one big movie scene.

We want to be seen,
We yell, and we scream;
Hoping for something,
That division can't bring...

It's all about living in-between.

Refusing to let them drive a wedge,
Pushing us off the edge.

ON'T EXCUSE

WE CAN REFUSE

F WE DON'T ACCUSE

IT'S UP **TO US TO CHOOSE.**

IT'S UP **TO US TO** CHOOSE

F WE **DON'T ACCUSE**

E CAN REFUSE

ON'T EXCUSE

Forgive every sin,
We are akin…

Kindred creatures,
Each other's teachers.

Stop playing preacher.
Stop being a screecher!

Over-dramatic,
Asymptomatic;
Time to try another tactic.

WE'VE LOST OUR WAY...

Look at it
Like this...

What would it be like,
If you learned that habit?

It's easy to judge,
Easier to hold a grudge...

We can try to nudge,
But think, maybe you misjudge?

Maybe, you were wrong all along.

Singing different songs;
Songs all the same...

Just different games,
Where each other blames.

ONLY HEARING WHAT WE SAY.

194

SHAME,

SHAME...

SHAME!

Crying shame…
Shame,
SHAME!

We have no clear aim;
We've forgotten we are all the same.

Shame!
Please cover up the name;
We're all to blame
For playing this game.

SHAME,

SHAME...

SHAME!

HOW DIFFERENT ARE WE?

Why can't we put aside our differences?
To see that we,
Have more in common than you think.

Why can't we?
Why can't we?

IMAGINE,
What would set us free;
From the hatred, we decide to be.

Free, free…
Imagine how that may be.

WE CAN'T EVEN SEE.

Walking light as a feather,
Able to weather any storm,
Making this our norm.

IMAGINE HOW THAT MAY BE

Rising above the clouds,
Soaring in the wind…

Like a bird,
Would that be so absurd?

IMAGINE HOW THAT MAY BE

Letting go of differences,
Make them inferences.

Flipping the script,
Reality ripped…

It flipped right over.

We see our commonalities,
Revealed in our personalities...

Strengthened by our capabilities,
To accept our own abilities.

By working together,
Not against each other...

Seeing others,
As sisters and brothers.

Hugging one another,
Removing that frown…

Enough with that dirty glance,
Giving everyone a chance…

To be kind;
To be love;
To be a dove...

To be forgiven,
For practicing no religion.

MAKE THE RIGHT DECISION.

TO END THE DIVISION.

END THE DIVISION.

END THE DIVISION.

END THE DIVISION.

End the division,
Make the right decision.

**End the division,
Make the right decision.**

END THE DIVISION.

END THE DIVISION.

END THE DIVISION.

TO END THE DIVISION.

MAKE THE RIGHT DECISION

THE PACIFIST

When other people are hurting,
They hurt others...

It's a vicious cycle.

The pacifist.

The pacifist has no list.

Enemy-free,
No judgment for thee.

The pacifist,
Brings stability to the fight...

Refusing to stoke the flames;
Unwilling to play games,
Placing blames.

The pacifists only aim,
To free others from their shame.

Tame their inner-beast,
At the least,
Sharing in a feast.

Working with each other,
Refusing to fight,
Or act contrite,
When it's not right.

CAN WE YELL?!

Sure, problems swell...

Oh well, Oh well...

What does the future foretell?

Anger spells,
Alarm bells...

Siren calls,
Inevitable falls.

FALLING,

FALLING,

FALLING.

LIFE, IS, STALLING.

LIFE, IS, STALLING

FALLING,

FALLING

FALLING.

The pacifiist tries to bring peace,
At the very least…

To push back against this angry beast.

Caving to craving;
Paving the path for friction,
To feed the addiction…

Ongoing confliction.

A changing condition,
Through attrition.

In time,
Pacifists turn the tide.

Bringing classes together,
Changing the weather.

From stormy to clear,
Coming together here...

The pacifist in near,
Let's revere.

The pacifist helps to steer,
Helping us share.

DENY,

DON'T TRY

AND DIE.

A LIE, GONE AWRY.

FLAMING, SHAMING, DEFAMED

UNDETTERED,

PAIN

OBSCURRED.

The pacifist knows,
Where anger goes.

In others eyes,
Evil glows,
At each close.

Poison spills,
Intoxication fills;
Curiosity thrills,
Hurt kills…

People's wills.

The will to live.
The power to forgive.

But, the pacifist still will give...

Another chance to overcome,
To be someone.

Free of suffering,
Mental pains;
Anguish,
Struggle too...

BRINGING EVERYONE OUT OF THE BLUE.

Facing adversity,
Through diversity.

Trying new things,
Seeing what that brings.

Accepting a challenge,
Bringing peace to tackle fear;
Showing how much they care,
Even when others may scare.

PAIN WILL CEASE...

PEACE WILL CREASE.

EVE, AND YOU SHA'LL REC

NOBODY CAN DECIEVE...

WHEN YOU ARE OPEN TO RECIEVE.

BELIEVE

BELIEVE

BELIEVE

The pacifist knows, and it shows.

When other people are hurting,
They hurt others too;
Make them believe things untrue,
Said about you.

The story grew...
And grew and grew.

A vicious cycle,
We feel a need to recycle.

The pacifist,
Is no perfectionist.

The pacifist,
Accepts nature's imperfections…

As perfections,
Intersections…

Crossing points,
Truth anoints.

NOTHING DISSAPOINTS.

Where there's imperfection,
There's only perfection.

Accepting things as they are,
Shining stars…

Like flashing cars,
Near or far.

The pacifist never spars…

The pacifist never picks at scars.

The pacifist accepts who we all are...

Perfectly imperfect...

Terrific,
Supercalifragilistic.

Able to reject pre-condition,
Through simple addition...

To reposition,
A changing condition.

Sharing peace,
Even as anger may increase.

Sending divine energy
To bring about synergy.

Feeling good,
Even when misunderstood.

Pacifism changes the prism of perception,
To see through deception,
Without exception...

Or so, the pacifist says.

WHAT IF...

WE INCREASED OUR PERSPECTIVE?

IN A BUBBLE

Present in our ways,
Unable to reset for days.

Where did we go?
Why can't we flow?

Faster, faster, faster…
WE ARE NO MASTER.

This bubble spells trouble.

Feeling trapped,
Energy zapped…

EVERY EMOTION OVERLAPPED.

An echoless chamber;
Sounds reverberate...

Our cries cannot escape.

Slowly, the bubble expands
Into parallel lands…

NOBODY UNDERSTANDS
WHAT IT DEMANDS...

How is it our reality stands?

IN A BUBBLE...
COMING TROUBLE.

HOW IS IT OUR REALITY STANDS?

Lifts true feeling,
Making life fulfilling.

Filling us with a way to justify our identity,
Day after day…

Unable to defy this social tie,
One big lie…

Too often until the day we die.

IN A BUBBLE...
PAIN WILL DOUBLE.

Lies, lies;
DESPICABLE LIES…

Hate defies, personifies.

It seems unwise,
That love can overcome;
Fear undone,
EGO slung...

Stops us from living on the run.

If only there were someone;
If only there were individuals…

Honest brokers,
Replacing pokers,
INCITEFUL STOKERS…

Lacking insight, despite what they might tell you.

If only there were people….

Trustful leaders,
Evil defeaters…

NOT ACTORS PLAYING THEATER WITH OUR LIVES.

IT'S ALL AN ACT...

LIGHTS,

CAMERA,

ACTION.

QUIT REACTING
TO THOSE WHO ARE ACTING.

Reality teeters on edge,
As the cult makes its pledge.

ACTION!

ACTION!

ACTION!

THERE IS NO COUNTERACTION.

A CONTRACTION,
ANOTHER DISTRACTION.

Sitting in movie theaters,
Watching...

As they string us along,
Making us feel like we belong.

Otherwise expelling…

Those who dare question?
Follow unquestionably…or else.

SUFFOCATING, LEFT WAITING.

Bringing chaos to their act,
Helping to distract;
As problems stack,
The world will crack.

Refusing to be controlled,
Patrolled by bad actors;
Enter new factors.

POP...

POP...

POP...

POP...

POP!

POP!

The bubble shakes,
Powerful words create;
Earthquakes,
As we awake…

TO A FUTURE AT STAKE.

READY,

AIM,

FIRE...

HELPING TO INSPIRE

Trying to pop,
Put a stop;
Too another bad cop…

Bad actors,
Utilizing universal factors.

POP...

POP...

POP...

POP...

POP!

POP!

Fighting for freedom,
Returning our kingdom;
Back to the people…

So peace can soar,
A winning score...

War no more,
The bubble tore.

PARANOIA DOUBLES

Amplification bubbles,
Paranoia doubles…

Distortion troubles,
Comprehension struggles.

Try understanding,
Things that aren't even there;
Unable to see clear,
Controlled by fear, paralysis scare.

Frozen in darkness,
Cold starkness…

Movement impossible.

Consider crazy possibilities,
What are the probabilities?

Perspective shrinks,
Poisoned drinks;
Truth stinks.

Running,
Hiding…

Reality sliding,
Illusion guiding.

Only in amplification bubbles;
Do we begin these troubles?

Where paranoia doubles,
Comprehension struggles.

Lacking trust, which is a must.

Settling dust, our brains rust.

Until a violent gust,
Make us go bust…

Take new routes;
Unleashed, past deceased.

Now, now, now;
If only we could allow,
Ourselves to enter **THE NOW.**

Bursting through bubbles,
Seeing through troubles;
Where paranoia doubles,
Minds left in rubbles.

CRUMBLING

FALLING,

STALLING…

EGO IS CALLING.

SUFFOCATING

NEVER

LIBERATING.

Torn apart,
From the reality part.

Trapped by;
Amplification, disassociation,
Bubbles that cause desecration.

Anger, fear;
Inability to see clear,
Or hear anything outside…

Where the universe opens wide,
Free to flow with the tide…

In and out,
Experiencing what life's about.

Free of the bubble
That's caused too much trouble.

Free of the bubble
That's caused too much trouble.

A CANCER ON SOCIETY

PEOPLE LACK SOBRIETY,

A CANCER ON SOCIETY.

INCESSANT

CHATTER...

A cancer on society,
People lack sobriety;
Looking to intoxicate,
Refusing to re-educate.

Isn't that great?

DARK

MATTER.

REFUSING TO RE-EDUCATE,

LOOKING TO INTOXICATE.

Getting lost,
No matter the cost.

Highs and lows,
Nobody knows...

One way grows,
Another one slows.

What it shows?
Nobody knows.

Nobody knows,
Nobody knows.

NOW SUPPOSE...

Now suppose...

Suppose,
Suppose.

You discover,
Uncover secrets...

Recover lost emotions,
Magic potions...

To make anything go,
To make everything glow...

To make time slow,
To go high not low.

WHERE

NOTHING

MATTERS.

Empty feelings become filling;
Empty feelings become thrilling;
Empty feelings become healing.

Emptiness is killing;
Left unwilling.

OUR

IDENTITY

SHATTERS.

Don't you want to seek the peak;
Take a peek?

Speak your mind,
Refuse to be blind...

Unwind from intoxication,
From lack of information…

Association with inadequate education.

Cancer, toxicity;
Dark matter, incessant chatter.

Where did all the laughter go?

When did you no longer grow;
Start moving fast instead of slow?

Will you ever know?
Will you ever know?

I hope so.
I hope so.

Kill the cancer, become the answer.

Don't wait until it's too late.

Be real. Heal.
Be real. Heal.

Kill the cancer, become the answer.

KILL THE CANCER...

A cancer on society,
People lack sobriety;
Looking to intoxicate,
Refusing to re-educate.

BECOME THE ANSWER.

INSANE, YOU SEE

TRAPPED...

TRAPPED...

TRAPPED...

OTENTIAL UNTAPPE

It's plain to me,
Insane, you see…

Trapped in a society,
Where we are made to feel free…

Even though that can't be;
How can it be?

HOW CAN IT BE?

HOW CAN IT BE?

HOW CAN IT BE?

PLAIN TO ME, INSANE YOU

From my perspective,
I see the great big sea;
Of tidal waves,
EGO craves...

Trapping our souls, creating gigantic holes.

TRAPPED...

TRAPPED...

TRAPPED...

OTENTIAL UNTAPPE

Stuck in currents;
Torrents of…

Shock,
Awe;
That which we saw…

UNIVERSAL LAW.

PLAIN *TO ME, INSANE* YOU SE

It's plain to me,
Insane, you see;
I'll make a plea,
You will not see...

Ruled by decree,
You are not free;
Trapped in a sea,
Told how to be.

MAKE A PLEA, NOBODY WILL S

Angry, Angry, Angry…
Blanketed by misery,
Caught up in history.

Struggling for survival,
Hoping for a revival…

Of our soul essence;
Of our existing presence.

TRAPPED...

TRAPPED...

TRAPPED...

OTENTIAL UNTAPPE

Breaking rough waters,
Bringing upon a sense of calm...

Relaxing the mind,
Helping it unwind...

Released from the bind,
Of everything timed.

It's plain to me,
Insane, you see;
Unable to be,
Understand what it means to be free...

From our society,
Lacking sobriety;
Ruled by anxiety,
A self-proclaimed deity.

Intoxicated with fear,
We fail to share;
No ability to see clear,
Evil actors steer.

They steer us…
This way and that.

They keep us…
In our habitat.

Upon us, they spat;
They called us stupid;
They called us fat.

"ARE YOU STUPID?!"

TRAPPED…

TRAPPED…

TRAPPED…

OTENTIAL UNTAPPED

TRAPPED...

TRAPPED...

TRAPPED...

OTENTIAL UNTAPPE

Polluted,
Obscured…
MIND DETTERED.

Crowded,
Shrouded...
MIND CLOUDED.

Blocked from truth;
We've become numbers in their game…

To them,
We're all the same;
But, only for their aim…

WE HAVE NO NAME.

IT IS INSANE.

HOW DO I EXPLAIN?

How can I explain,
What goes on in this brain?

How can I explain,
Without having to strain?

How can I explain?
How can I explain?

How can I explain,
Without sounding insane?

Making an effort,
Trying my best...

Putting every bit of patience I have,
To the test.

Pushing,
Pulling;
Overruling.

Striving forwards,
Striving towards…

UNDERSTANDING.

Landing on two feet,
Continuing down this one-way street;
Unwilling to repeat,
Admit defeat…

Left to repeat,
I've never tried to be discrete.

My intentions are to treat,
Situations single-handedly...

Giving my full undivided attention,
Opening myself to ascension.

Dividing,
Separating from the whole;
Creating a hole,
Where interpretation stole...

Me from the here and now;
Lacking rest,
I failed the test.

WHERE?

WHAT?

WHY?

WHEN?

HOW?

I make no demand,
As I try to understand.

As I try to explain,
I often feel insane.

I don't want to complain,
But, how do I explain?

HOW DO I EXPLAIN?

HOW DO I EXPLAIN?

HOW DO I EXPLAIN?

HOW DO I EXPLAIN?

HOW DO I EXPLAIN

I UNDERSTAND. I DO.

I UNDERSTAND. I DO.

We can whine,
We can complain...

We can create the stain,
Left on our brain.

Insane, insane,
Malfunctioning mainframe;
Others to blame,
For us living in shame.

While you whine and complain,
Allow me to explain...

Allow me to explain,
Why you've been driven insane.

I UNDERSTAND. I DO.

It's plain to me,
Insane, you see…

Do you see?
DO YOU SEE?

You're getting angry.

Straining to see,
Incapability.

Unable,
Unstable;
This mindset, inescapable.

Wavering back and forth,
South to North…

Up and down,
Left with a frown…

THE WHOLE WORLD FLIPPED UPSIDE DOWN.

THERE

IS NO

UNDERSTANDING

THERE

IS ONLY

REPRIMANDING.

Questioning your worth,
Giving birth to uncertainty…

THERE IS NO CLARITY,
Room for charity.

*Whining and complaining
Constantly defaming...*

*Blaming others;
Accepting no responsibility,
Lost in instability…*

*Forgetting you have little ability,
For tranquility.*

*Whining and complaining,
Overstraining.*

*Trying hard,
To disregard.*

ISN'T IT MYSTERIOUS,

OW SERIOUS THINGS SEEM TO BE

Isn't it mysterious,
How serious things seem to be?

Isn't it strange,
This constant change?

ISN'T IT STRANGE,

THIS CONSTANT CHANGE?

Lacking rationality,
Understanding….

Demanding people look,
Commanding them to listen…

Stuck in a condition,
Of unwavering position.

Numerous complaints,
Even more grievances…

Baggage weighing you down.

Carrying such a big load,
Taking the bumpy road.

It doesn't bode well,
Trapped in a shell…

A living hell,
Within an evil spell...

BELIEVING EVERYTHING THEY SELL.

Oh well, oh well,
Here's what I foretell.

HERE'S WHAT I FORTELL...

Singing an ode of sadness,
As you whine and complain;
An endless stain,
Driving you insane.

Refraining from any attempts
At explaining...

What's going on,
This broken song…

IT'S JUST PLAIN WRONG.

WHY DO WE HOLD ON?

Triggered by the littlest thing...

What it may bring,
Suffering.

Frustration,
Indoctrination;
Accusation,
Insinuation…

**There's never any inspiration,
Room for interpretation.**

WHY CAN'T WE LET GO?

TO WHAT

DO

WE OWE?

Victimhood,
Never understood.

Victimhood.
Stiff as wood.

Lacking any perspective to see.
Lacking any perspective to break-free.

Believe me.
I understand,
I do.

I understand. I DO.

I UNDERSTAND. I DO.

WHAT IF...

WE WERE HONEST?

HONESTLY

WHY DO WE DENY...

It's tough being honest.
But, honesty is the best policy.

Honestly,

Gently...

Deceptively,

Insincerely.

The honest truth can be tough to hear,
Release your fear so that you can share.

INSTEAD OF FLY?

LOVE

DON'T

LIE...

LOVE DON'T LIE,
DON'T LET TRUTH STAND-BYE.

DON'T LET

TRUTH

STAND-BYE.

Feel comfortable,
Opening up…

Your heart,
Your soul…

Untruths have stole.

They stole,
They stole,
They stole.

They stole TIME,
They stole OPPORTUNITY…

TO MAKE IT ALL INTERTWINE…

To learn the ability,
Of agility.

They stole minutes,
Seconds…

They stole days,
Hours…

They stole months,
Weeks…

They stole years and years and years…

THEY STOLE LIFETIMES.

YOU LIE,

YOU DIE,

YOU WATCH...

LIFE PASS BYE.

And, who cares?
Nobody seems to.

Trapped by lies,
We should despise;
They make us unwise.

Never learning what it means to be true,
HONEST TOO;
Misled by the few….

AND THEN,

YOU ASK...

WHY?

AT THE TOP,

T
R
I
C
K
L
I
N
G

D
O
W
N...

THESE MASSES, THEY DROWN.

WHY?

WHY?

WHY?

WHY?

WHY?

HONESTLY, HONESTY…
TO BE COMPLETELY HONEST.

Honestly,
That's how I strive to be,
Honesty is the best policy.

HONESTY

BE HONEST.

BE REAL,

EXPRESS

HOW YOU FEEL.

I BELIEVE IN HONESTY,
Such a travesty when one lacks integrity...

THE CONCEPT OF TENSEGRITY,
A connected system most fail to see.

BE HONEST.

BE REAL,

THAT IS

HOW WE HEAL.

WHAT DO YOU BELIEVE?

I rest in my ability,
Ground myself in tranquility;
Released from past fragility,
I've rediscovered stability.

ARE YOU ABLE TO RECIEVE?

WHAT DOES IT MEAN TO BE HONEST?

To never steal,

To feel real;

To heal…

Peeling back layers

REJECTING NAYSAYERS…

They are traitors.

Here we can find and heal our mind.

Here we can unwind in space untimed.

THE TRUTH WE CAN CONCIEVE

Released from past trauma,

From melodrama;

INSOMNIA, VISIONS OF DYSTOPIA.

Disoriented, bewildered, confused;

OUR MIND ABUSED, SO OFTEN MISUSED.

SOMEWHERE

IN THE

MIDDLE...

Someone accused,
Another blamed;
OTHERS SHAMED,
Engulfed, Inflamed.

WE SOLVE

THE UNIVERSAL

RIDDLE.

At some point, we become trapped.

Caught by surprise,
Caught up in lies.

Caught off guard,
By a fractured shard…

Of glass…broken…unawoken…unspoken.

SILENCE BECOMES OUR ALLIANCE

RELIANT ON BEING SILENT.

Falling into place in outer space;
Watching **EGO** replace,
Leaving its trace.

As our soul disappears,
WHO CARES?

IS THIS A CURSE?

Blown off course,
By a powerful force...

Into an empty universe,
HOW DO WE REVERSE?

ANOTHER BLANK VERSE.

VAST AND WIDE,
INFINITE PLACES TO HIDE.

IDENTITIES STOLEN,
BRAINS SWOLLEN.

AHHHH!

STOP!

POP.

AHHHH!

STOP!

POP.

PEACE TAKEN FROM US
WITH DISHONESTY...

SUCH A TRAVESTY,
A SAD STORY...

Yet, the story of too many.

WHAT DOES THE WORLD NEED?

WHAT DOES THE WORLD NEED?

What does the world need?
What does the world need?

What does it need,
How can we feed?

So many seeds,
Stuck in weeds.

No one to lead,
Away from greed.

Trying to save,
Situation grave.

Intoxication paves,
Our environment caves.

What does the world need?
What does the world need?

What does it need,
How can we breathe?

TIME

SPED...

NEVER

GETTING AHEAD

Rising tide,
Storms so wide;
They lied,
People cried.

Carbon thieves,
Who believes;
Pollution breeds,
Our planet bleeds.

SEAS

OF RED...

LIVING

DEAD.

What does the world need?

What does the world need?

What does it need,
Someone to lead…

Then it can be freed,
Changing speed.

LIGHTING ANOTHER WAY,

EVERY SINGLE DAY...

TIL DARKNESS GOES AW

What it needs is someone...

What it needs is someone...
Someone to lead.

That's what the world needs.

T'S WHAT **THE** WORLD NEE

THE WORLD I SEE

INCREDIBLY

THE WORLD

I SEE,

IS FREE...

Incredibly the world I see,
Is free of curiosity.

Incredibly the world I see,
Is free of curiosity.

Free of curiosity,
Eliminating what could be...

EVERY POSSIBILITY.

FREE

OF CURIOSITY,

ELIMINATING

WHAT COULD BE.

Accepting what those in power have told,
The millions of lies they've sold.

It's an old story…

Historical in nature;
Asking rhetorical questions;
They know the answers...

THEY CREATE THEM.

The rich and powerful,
Predators attack;
Feasting on souls,
Sharks hunting...

In warm waters, they swarm.

Our leaders punting,
Our current problems,
Past and present;
Making for an unpleasant future.

It's a feeding frenzy;
Full of envy..

**Hunger driven by
A desire for power.**

**Win at all costs,
Friendly competition lost.**

CONTROLLED.

MANIPULATED.

UNDERAPPRECIATED.

We are controlled.
We are manipulated.
WE ARE UNDERAPPRECIATED.

Yet, we've made our beds
With these bedfellows...

Full of hollow promises,
TO TACKLE <u>THE ISSUES OF THE DAY</u>...

And another one has gone away,
While these problems stay.

These politicians pray,
For show and play...

THEY NEVER HAVE TO PAY.

THEY NEVER HAVE TO PAY.

Until the next calamity,
Shatters our very own humanity.

Resulting from mass delusions,
Reaching unreasonable conclusions...

COLLUSIONS WITH THE DEVIL,
CONFUSIONS OF THE MIND,
CAUGHT IN A BIND,
LETTING OURSELVES BE DEFINED.

WE WERE TOO AFRAID, TO UNITE AND REBEL.

Under the banner of a mass movement,
FOR IMPROVEMENT...

Leading to a destructive spell,
AS DEMOCRACY FELL.

DESTRUCTION

REDUCTION...

CORROSION,

EXPLOSION!

BOOM!

BOOM!

BOOM!

CONSUME,

DOOM..

SPREADING GLOOM

CRUMBLING,
CRASHING,
IMPLODING;
Each institution eroding.

FROM THE INSIDE OUT,
SOCIETY IN DOUBT.

CREDIBLY THIS IS WHAT I SEE

As these sharks watch on,
Freedom gone...

C'mon C'mon,
Weapons drawn.

Incredibly this is what I see,
People lack curiosity.

Spawning hate,
Dooming fate...

WHEN WILL IT ABATE?
THE WORLD CAN'T WAIT.

PEOPLE LACK CURIOSITY.

ON TOP OF EVERYTHING,
THESE ACTORS CREATE CHAOTIC FACTORS;
WRITING DARK CHAPTERS...

We choose to accept.

Suffering at their hands,
Pulled by their demands.

Stirred by their words,
TO BECOME DISTURBED...

Like daggers,
Like swords...

WEAPONIZED MADNESS.

Accepting deception,
Living inception;
An open reception,
For insurrection.

Incredibly the world these people see,
Is free of curiosity...

As they claim innocence,
WITH THEIR COGNITIVE DISSONANCE...

WHERE IS THE RESISTANCE?

Why the persistance?
Why the insistance?

Conditioning, repositioning...

Losing our mind,
Turning blind,
Stuck on rewind.

ET'S GO BACK

OFF TRACK

EELING LACK...

CRACK!

RETRACT.

WITHOUT FACT.

WHY

CAN'T WE

SEE...

WHAT

HEY'VE MADE U

OUT TO BE?

Lurking at the edge,
Bad ideas wedge...

Dividing masses,
As time passes.

Incredibly the world I see,
Is free of curiosity...

Free of curiosity,
Eliminating what could be...

EVERY POSSIBILITY.

THE TRUTH

IS ANYTHING TRUE?

CAN WE SEE THROUGH?

Do I witness the truth?
Or, do I abstract the truth?

Can I be the self-witness,
To see beyond myself?

OUR STORY GREW...

UNTIL THAT'S ALL WE KNEW.

Talk is cheap,
Most act like sheep...

Being led,
Being fed…

Living dead,
Life sped.

Talk has stopped,
Reasons flopped.

Replaced by doing...

Always going,
Never slowing.

Accomplishing feats,
Each repeats...

Time slows until it goes;
As true personality grows,
Our essence glows.

SLOWING...

SLOWING...

SLOWING...

SOON WILL BE GLOWING.

GROWING...

GROWING...

MING AND GOIN

A worldly identity,
Self-proclivity...

Who we've come to be,
REALITY.

Watching we will see…

Observing,
Preserving…

Dignity,
Until infinity...

Making this
Our holy trinity.

WE ARE THE SAME...

We are the same,
In this game of life.

OUR AIM,
IS THE SAME.

Peace,
Released from desires…

Internal fires.

Violence ceases...

It appeases, it pleases.

The search for something,
That's been here all along.

The whole time,
Missing sign after sign...

Preferring to whine,
When it could be fine.

GROWING ASKEW AS TIME FLEW

AMSISING EVERY SINGLE CLUE

Refusing to act,
To counteract;
Fill a void we lacked,
Problems stacked.

One on top of the other...

Towering above,
Hiding our potential to love.

We stoodbye unable to fly,
Holding onto our tie, another lie...

Until one day we die,
And we ask the question as to why?

So, here's the question...
Do I witness or abstract the truth?

WHAT IS TRUE?

EVERY LAST THING

EVERY LAST THING...

Every thought is shot,
Every last feeling caught;
Everything I've been taught,
Sits in my mind, making it slowly rot.

What have I bought with my time?

Why has life
Felt like such a crime?

How come we abuse, refuse,
Make ourselves lose?

Waiting for a fuse to break,
Igniting a ticking bomb…

Bringing fire to the night.

Ending our plight,
A constant fight,
Hiding light.

CONNECTED BY A STRING.

Struggling for survival,
Upside down revival.

Stuck on a page,
With each war we wage.

Watching truth sit in a cage,
As deception takes center stage.

Drawing attention,
Causing dissension…

From rank and file,
As they try to defile; rile…

Stir up anxiety,
Rangel society…

CLOAKED BY PIETY,
Masses have no room for variety.

Groupthink needs to sink in,
Until the future feels grim…

Independence thins,
EGO WINS.

ME SPINS AND SPINS AND SPINS

SPINNING OUT OF CONTROL.

ON A ROLL, IT TAKES A TOLL.

There's no room for a minority,
To give in to authority;
A controlling seniority.

Populations become ruled,
Decisions overruled...

Choice disappears,
Voicelessness appears....

Insecurity tears.
COMPOUNDING FEARS.

No name,
No comfort…

We become the same,
We live in shame.

A cult has formed,
As our humanity's deformed...

EVERYONE UNDERPERFORMED.

WHY...

WHY...

WHY?

I WONDER...

WONDER.

I WONDER WHY?

I wonder…
I wonder why…

I WONDER WHY
WE DENY…

WHAT STARES US STRAIGHT
IN THE EYE.

WHY...

WHY...

WHY?

WONDER.

I WONDER...

I WONDER WHY?

Drawn by sounds,
Alluring words…

LED ASTRAY,
DAY BY DAY; BY DAY BY DAY…

BY DAY…

BY DAY…

BY DAY!

Seductive,
Instructive,
Inductive…

RECONSTRUCTIVE.

LOST IN GRAY,…..

BREATH HELD AT BAY…

THERE'S NOTHING WE CAN SAY

INDUCED INTO A CULTISH WAY…
Groupthink rules the day,
Independence goes away.

I WONDER WHY...

PAYING TRIBUTE,
TO EVERY LOST ATTRIBUTE...

This loss at first feels acute,
Before time allows it to contribute...

TO BRAINWASHING,
Glossing over;
WHAT'S TRULY IMPORTANT.

CONNECTION,
RATHER THAN DEFLECTION.

Ignoring truth;
IGNORING SIMPLICITY;
ACCEPTING DUPLICITY.

I WONDER WHY?

I wonder why…
Why did we fall for this DECEPTION,
NAKED INCEPTION?

REJECTING TRUTH FOR LIES,
WATCHING HOPE AS IT DIES...

Led by fear in disguise,
Through a loving guise.

Falling for a ruse
It does confuse;
Allows **EGO** to choose,
Left to lose.

WHY...

WHY...

WHY?

WONDER.

I WONDER...

I WONDER WHY?

294

I WONDER WHY...

WHY...

WHY...

WHY?

I WONDER...

WONDER

I WONDER WHY?

So, I ponder this…
Wonder why so many believe this…

LIE,
STARING THEM STRAIGHT BACK IN THE EYE.

I WONDER WHY...

I WONDER WHY?

APPEARANCES

IS

IT

CLEAR?

I'd like to discuss APPEARANCES.

How often
Do our own eyes DECEIVE US?

How often
Is what we see, WHAT WE GET?

Is it because of what we see,
THAT WE GET SOMETHING ELSE
ENTIRELY?

CAN

THEY

HEAR?

IS

ANYONE

SINCERE?

Removed from sobriety...
A HIGHER SOCIETY.

False appearances…
A DECEPTION INCEPTION.

Pictures flipped upside down,
Twisted around,
Buried underneath the ground.

Confounded by surface appearances,
Misled by previous experiences.

Memory recollections,
Treasured collections;
Of inflection points,
Where truth disappoints.

DOES

ANYBODY

CARE?

Which leads me to the appearance;
AN APPEARANCE...

FALSE or TRUE,
Who really knew?

Who really knew?
Maybe you...

Maybe me...
Could it be who we see?

Reality...
Reality...

In actuality,
What we do see...

FALSE APPEARANCES,
REASSURANCES...

Fed images we want to see,
Rather than reality.

Appearing,
Disappearing...

Then reappearing;
However which way we want.

Will it continue to haunt?
What do we want?

APPEARANCES.

CAPABILITIES

WE ARE CAPABLE...

What are we capable of?
What limits, what we can and can't do?

WHY DO WE LIMIT OURSELVES?

Placing limitations,
Preventing new creations;
FOR WHAT?

Assimilation.
SO WE CAN FIT IN.

This is where it all begins...

A lack of discipline...

Watching as the world spins,
As our understanding thins.

WE ARE CAPABLE...

ARE WE CAPABLE?

Awash in the ether,
Lost in the benign...

Time unwinds,
Future binds.

Flipped on its head,
We've been misled…

The things they fed,
What we should dread.

A frozen bed...

Rock hard,
Surface scarred,
Knowledge tarred.

Capabilities restricted,
Over-conflicted...

Easily scripted,
Already convicted...

SOCIETY AFFLICTED.

ARE WE CAPABLE?

WHAT'S

STOPPING

US?

Limiting possibilities,
Sacrificing abilities;
FOR WHAT?

TO BELONG,
For what we long for…

For group identity,
A predictable reality…

When in actuality,
Matter of factuality…

What type of reality is this?

WHAT'S

STOPPING

US?

Think of all the things you'll miss.

From the unpredictable,
To the despicable…

THE BLANK ROAD AHEAD.

One where life is never dead,
Where **EGO's** never fed…

Lies they said,
Have no street cred…

Where chance led,
Instead, instead.

BLINKING

ERTHINKING

SINKING

INKING,

WHAT WERE

WE THINKING?

WE ARE CAPABLE...

DON'T

STOP...

DON'T

MOVE...

DON'T

TRY TO IMPROVE.

What are we capable of?
What are we capable of?

If we can be honest,
We are capable of anything.

ARE CAPABLE OF ANYTHIN

305

WHAT IF...

WE BROKE-FREE?

FLY AWAY

Discipline dissolves,
Anxiety revolves,
My mind evolves...

To solve a lifelong mystery
Which is our history.

FLY AWAY...

FLY AWAY...

I SAY, I SAY...

FLY AWAY..

FLY AWAY...

I SAY,

It's when I'm tired,
Habits are wired...

Engrained and stained,
Over-trained.

Parts of identity,
Others fail to see...

And, all I want is to be free...

Free of this toxicity;
Opening me, potentially.

Untapped,
Currently trapped…

Waiting to be released;
WAITING TO BE UNLEASHED.

FLY AWAY...

FLY AWAY.

I SAY, I SAY...

Like butterflies, awakening,
Breaking out of their cocoons;
Spreading their wings,
Flying away….

NO LONGER FORCED TO STAY,
DAY AFTER DAY AFTER DAY.

FLY AWAY..

FLY AWAY...

I SAY.

Today is the day
To pave the way...

To pave the way,
And fly away.

FLY AWAY...

FROM A DIVIDED WAY.

From these wings,
Hope springs...

Tied to no strings,
Empty-things.

Feeling this air,
Witnessing it clear.

Tiredness,
Sluggishness goes,
ENERGY GLOWS

As thought slows,
The soul knows....

What is good,
What is bad,
What makes us mad!

A disciple of discipline,
Forgiving a history of sin...

Breathing out anxiety for sobriety.

Discovering unlimited ability for stability.

Flying away...
From a divided way.

A DIVIDING LINE

THIS LIFE

OF

MINE...

A dividing line,
THIS LIFE OF MINE...

On one side I'm fine,
On the other I whine…

WHY IS IT SO HARD TO SHINE?

A

DIVIDING

LINE.

With division comes revision,
Edited like television...

Oblivion of sorts,
Movie shorts.

Why can't I see, it's cutting me;
Into pieces, many pieces?

Pieces hard to match,
Too easily scratched...

Snatching from the hand of God,
Admiration for this creation.

DIVIDE,

DIVIDE...

PICK

A SIDE...

I KNOW

THEY LIED.

OUTSIDE,

TO TIED...

INSIDE,

OU TRIED..

E COULD

NOT DECIDE.

INSTEAD, WE ARE SPILLING BLOOD;
DROWNING IN A FLOOD;
STUCK IN MUD.

THUD! THUD! THUD! THUD!

Killing for a thrilling second,
GONE INSTANTANEOUSLY.

Between this dividing line,
THIS LINE OF MINE...

Here I'm fine,
There I whine....

IN THE MIDDLE, I SHINE.

It's hard to find;
Find peace of mind.

It's harder to keep it when you find it.
Sustaining this bliss, easy to miss.

A DIVIDING LINE...

Retaining an ability to abstain,
From pleasure, from pain...

An incessant desire,
Catching fire...

Choosing to retire,
From being a liar;
For truth to take us higher.

A DIVIDING LINE...

Retaining an ability to obtain,
All there is to gain;
When we can refrain,
From desires drain.

There's a fleeting moment in time;
Gone forever, never to be held again.

Here it began,
WITH NO PLAN.

Here it ended,
WE RE-INVENTED.

IN THE MIDDLE...

On a dividing line,
THIS LINE OF MINE...

In the middle,
Answers a universal riddle.

Answers come and go,
What we know,
Time will show.

HERE *IS* **WHERE WE GLOW**

CHOREOGRAPHY

COLOR-BLIND,

OUR PATHS ALIGNED...

Choreography,
It's like geography.

Finding this place,
Discovering your pace...

Expanding space,
Together as a race.

IN THE MIDDLE...

AN ANSWER TO OUR RIDDLE

Color-blind,
Our paths aligned...

**Together we shined,
As one-kind.**

TOGETHER WE SHINED,

AS ONE-KIND.

IN A TRANCE,

BY CHANCE...

THE DANCE,

Consciously,
Connectively...

Objectively,
With integrity.

Choreography,
Internal geography.

Channeling pathways,
Navigating through…

Connecting to,
What can only be true.

Choreography,
External geography.

RESTART,

PARTING WAYS,

FROM MINDLESS WAYS,

COLOR-BLIND,

OUR PATHS ALIGNED...

Outside in,
What has this been?

Inside out,
What comes about?

Whether we like it or not,
We become what we are taught...

Not a single thought,
Has not been bought...

A choreographic shot,
That is how we fought.

Choreography,
The world will be.

Choreography,
It's like geography.

TOGETHER WE SHINED,

AS ONE-KIND.

WHY CAN'T THE WORLD BE?

This world we see,
Lost in the sea...

Of emotion,
Commotion,
Constant motion.

Why can't the world be,
Why can't we see?

Why can't it be,
Full of generosity?

Why can't it be,
Full of peace?

Why can't the world be,
Why can't we see?

Why can't it be,
WHY CAN'T IT BE?

Why can't it be,
Full of joy?

Why can't it be,
Full of laughter...

FROM HERE UNTIL THEREAFTER?

WHY CAN'T THE WORLD BE?

IT CAN BE.

IT CAN BE.

IT CAN BE.

IT CAN BE.

Why can't the world be,
What can't we see?

IT CAN BE.

IT CAN BE.

IT CAN BE.

IT CAN BE.

WHY CAN'T THE WORLD BE

But, it can be,
Can't you see?

It can be,
FREE.

It can be,
HAPPY.

**It can be,
What we want it to be.**

We make the world;
We shake the world;
We are the world.

WE ARE THE WORLD.

WE ARE THE WORLD.

WE ARE THE WORLD.

WE ARE THE WORLD.

WE ARE THE WORLD.

WE ARE THE WORLD.

UNBOUND

UNBOUND

UNBOUND...

UNBOUND...

Unbound…
Where we are found.

Unbound…
Where we are crowned.

Unbound…
We come out of the ground.

Unbound…
We heal any wound.

Unbound…
Everyone comes around.

UNBOUND

UNBOUND...

UNBOUND...

Here,
Everything ties together…

Including the weather.

Your actions,
Mine…

They connect in a line;
Easy to see, hard to define.

We will be fine,
If we observe each sign.

UNBOUND.

UNBOUND...

UNBOUND...

UNBOUND..

UNBOUND.

UNBOUND...

A SYMPHONY OF SOUND.

A SYMPHONY OF SOUND.

UNBOUND...

UNBOUND.

UNBOUND...

UNBOUND.

UNBOUND...

UNBOUND...

PLACING ZERO LIMITATIONS,
AS TO OUR IMAGINATIONS.

ALLOWING FOR CREATIONS,
BEYOND NATIONS.

Free from control,
Rediscovering what **EGO** stole...

OUR SOUL.

Unbound...
Unbound....

WE ARE FINALLY FOUND.

IMAGINE LIFE

IMAGINE

LIFE...

WHAT IT

WOULD BE LIKE.

Imagine what life would be like...

What life would be like if we all felt alike...

The differences we could not strike...

Bang, bang, bang,
It's all so lame.

WHY

ARE WE

PLAYING

THIS GAME?

331

WHO

IS TO

BLAME?

What makes us unique,
Makes us a freak;
Much to seek,
Illuminating streak...

How come people make us feel so weak?

Every time we try to speak;
A soulful leak, echoing off a peak.

WE ARE

ONE IN THE

SAME.

If only, if only,
We weren't so lonely.

If only we could live truthfully...

Speak powerfully,
Instead of cowardly.

We try to be heard,
Only to become part of the herd...

It's all absurd,
This life assured...

So disturbed.

SHAME...

SHAME...

SHAME!

Doomed, thrown into darkness.

Spiraling; around and around,
Underneath oily ground...

Drowning our most hopeful sound.

To this, we are bound,
Creativity left unfound.

IMAGINE LIFE...

WHAT IT COULD BE LIKE.

If only, if only;
Our differences set us apart,
While letting us play our part...

We could have a fresh start,
To restart, create fine art.

Letting truth speak,
Ringing from peak to peak...

Flowing from creek to creek,
Into an elemental streak.

Accept that, live that, preach that.

Uniqueness is free; light, bright,
A most beautiful sight...

We don't need to feel alike,
Imagine what life would be like.

WHAT LIFE COULD BE LIKE...

WE DIDN'T HAVE TO FEEL ALIKE

Imagine what the world could be,
Imagine if we all were free.

INE, IMAGINE, IMAGINE US FR
GINE, IMAGINE, IMAGINE US

Free of fragility,
Free to regain stability.

Free of shame,
Free of taking blame.

We are one in the same,
Why take aim?

Tame the mental beast,
Enjoy life's feast.

To say the least…

Imagine, Imagine,
SIMPLY IMAGINE.

WOULDN'T THAT BE GREAT.
WOULDN'T THAT BE GREAT?

WOULDN'T THAT BE GREAT?

WOULDN'T THAT BE GREAT.

WOULDN'T IT BE GREAT IF...

WOULDN'T IT BE GREAT IF...

Wouldn't it be great if...

WE

COULD

DO

MORE,

Desire-less...

Not have to constantly impress.

Impress upon,

Become a pawn...

These moments gone.

Wouldn't it be great if...

We could clean up this mess...

Undress lies,

Easy to disguise.

If we could confess,

Settle for less...

Understanding less is more,

When we come ashore.

THAT WOULD BE GREAT!

WOULDN'T

IT BE

GREAT IF...

Wouldn't it be great if...

WE COULD BE
GREAT-FULL...

WE COULD BE
MORE TASTE-FULL...

Full of knowledge
We can acknowledge.

No school or college necessary;
Recognizing them, as an accessory.

Life becomes our most effective tool,
Living under no single rule...

THIS WOULD BE SO COOL,
And it would keep us full.

THAT

WOULD BE

GREAT!

Wouldn't it be great if…

WE COULD
SHOW COMPASSION…

MAKE CHANGE OUR PASSION,
An impermanent fashion.

Showing appreciation
With no denigration…

To bring about elation,
Making each moment a celebration.

IMAGINE…

IMAGINE…

IMAGINE…

IMAGINE…

MPLY IMAGIN

Wouldn't that be great?

Wouldn't that be great?

THAT WOULD BE GREAT!

THAT WOULD BE GREAT!

EPILOGUE

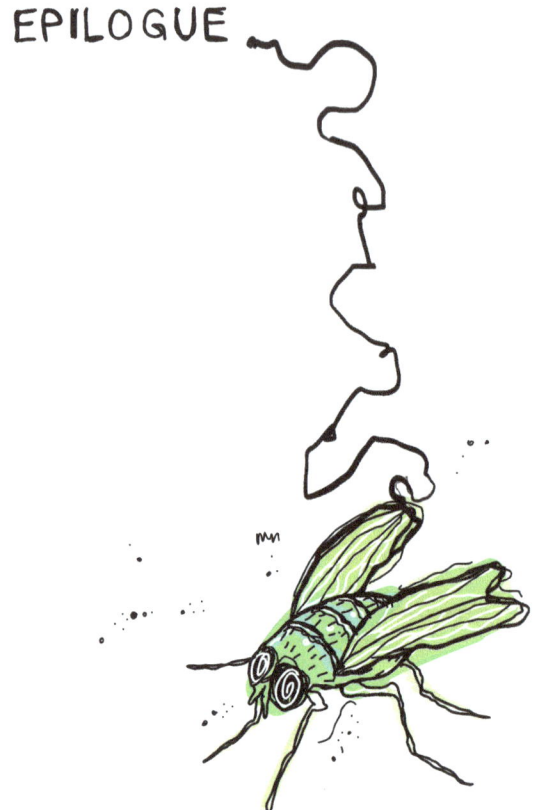

A LIGHT AT THE END OF THE TUNNEL

There's a light at the end of the tunnel,
Opposite of a black hole funnel.

Darkness doesn't stay inside;
On the other side,
Light does reside.

Often to sucked in,
This possibility feels thin...

Afraid of taking a spin,
You can never win.

Often...
Often...

If we start to soften...

Open our minds and listen...

We see there's a light at the end,
Where time can bend...

To the future or past,
It will outlast.

The light doesn't feel bright right away...
Once found, it is here to stay.

Growing stronger moment by moment.

Once like a stranger,
Change felt full of danger...

Until darkness is expelled;
Until it is banished...

We hope for it to vanish.

There is a light at the end of the tunnel.

I'M STILL DREAMING

Wouldn't it be great if...

Wars did not exist,
If we could coexist.

Wouldn't it be great if...

We could resist,
Not let evil persist.

The world is ours
Full of scars, part of stars.

We can fight,
Or we can unite.

We can find light,
Or settle for night.

"In 1996 at the age of 6,
I wrote my first poem,
Wouldn't it be great if..."

Wouldn't it be great if...

There was peace all arond the world
And friendes all arond the world.

Wouldn't it be great if...

Nobody got hurt and nobody used drugs.

Wouldn't it be great if...

Everybody had a smile on their face and
Everybody wore a helmet when skatebording and biking.

Wouldn't it be great if...

Everybody was helthy and
Everybody was a winner because they just tried their hardest.

And that would be great.

Ingram Content Group UK Ltd.
Milton Keynes UK
UKHW050636090523
421393UK00004B/15

9 781735 355443